POWER OF FORGIVENESS AND RECONCILIATION

Forgiveness is the sunrise of reconciliation

HOLLIS L. GREEN

A division of
GLOBALEDADVANCE PRESS

Power of Forgiveness And Reconciliation
Forgiveness is the Sunrise of Reconciliation

Copyright © 2020 by Hollis L. Green
Library of Congress Control Number: 2020903981

Green, Hollis L.,1933–
Power of Forgiveness and Reconciliation
ISBN 978-1-950839-06-3
Subject Codes and Description: Subject Codes and Description: 1: REL012100: Religion: Christian Life - Relationships
2: REL012120: Religion: Christian Living - Spiritual Growth
3: REL012110: Religion: Christian Living - Social Issues.

All rights reserved, including the right to reproduce this book or any part thereof in any form, except for inclusion of brief quotations in a review, without the written permission of GlobalEdAdvancePRESS.

Cover by GlobalGraphics

Photograph at sunrise by Gloria G. Green

City of publication: Nashville

Printed in Australia, Brazil, France, Canada, China, EU, Germany, Italy, Poland, Russia, Spain, UK, (3 sites)USA, and available on the Espresso Book Machine© worldwide. The Press does not have ownership of the contents of a book; this is the author's work and the author owns the copyright. All theory, concepts, constructs, and perspectives are those of the author and not necessarily the Press. They are presented for open and free discussion of the issues involved. All comments and feedback should be directed to the Email: [*comments4author@aol.com*] and the comments will be forwarded to the author for response.

Order books from www.gea-books.com/bookstore, on the Espresso Book Machine©, or any place good books are sold.

Published by
GreenWine Family Books™
A division of
GlobalEdAdvancePress

DEDICATION

This book is dedicated

"TO WHOM IT MAY CONCERN"

You may be known only to God, but each mature person has the God-given capability to forgive others. This broad dedication includes you, the Reader. Life is filled with difficult relationships and circumstances where you will have people to forgive and with whom you need to reconcile. *If you have difficulty following through with forgiveness, use the contents of this book and in the eyes of God you are priceless, because God has confidence in you!

---

*4. but let it be the beautification of the heart that will not fade away, even a calm and teachable spirit, which in God's eyes is priceless. (1 Peter 3:4 EDNT)

Contents

Preface		*God-like Power in Forgiveness*	9
Introduction		*"To err is human…!"*	13
1	APPROVAL and READINESS for Spiritual Growth		21
2	RESPECT and FORGIVENESS of Self and Others		27
3	AFFECTION and TOGETHERNESS in the Family		41
4	ATTITUDE and ACTION in Missional Lifestyle		61
5	PEACE and HARMONY during the Collect		77
6	PRAYER and RENUNCIATION in Confession		85
7	EXAMINATION and SOLIDARITY at Communion		97
8	TOGETHERNESS and FAITHFULNESS in Worship		115
9	TRANSPARENCY and RESTORATION with Believers		123
10	HARMONY and WITNESS in the Workplace		133
11	GENTLENESS and LONG-SUFFERING with the Lost		141
12	LOVE and FORGIVENESS for Enemies		149
Afterwords By First Readers		*"…to forgive is divine!"*	157
About The Author			159
Appendix A		*An Obituary for Common Sense*	161
Appendix B		*Theology of the Sweat Cloth*	163
Appendix C		*The "Together-Strong" NETWORK*	167
Appendix D		*Wound Wash*	171
Appendix E		*The Power Series*	177
Appendix F		*Steps to Spiritual Guidance*	179
Appendix G		*Affirmation of the Marriage Vows*	183
Appendix H		*Relevant Books by the Author*	187
Selected Reference Bibliography			191

> The power in forgiveness is the divine enablement which provides believers the capacity to examine themselves, correct their part in any dispute, and forgive and restore good relations with others.

Preface

God-like Power in Forgiveness

Forgiveness is the sunrise of reconciliation. The power to forgive the wrongdoings of others is an apparent capability divinely furnished believers as a tool to assist the maturation of individuals and harmony among family, friends and associates. It was a part of the Divine Plan to maintain harmony among families and the assembled believers in worship and outreach. Forgiving others is a vital part of maintaining a relationship with God and others. Forgiveness is needed to keep relationships current and transparent.

Nonetheless, the old saying, *"To err is human; to forgive is divine"* implies to promptly forgive the offenses and wrongdoing of others requires a spark of divinity, a jolt of reality and a moment of reasoned maturity. The author of a high school textbook attempting to explain the power of the A/H-bombs dropped at the end of World War II had difficulty finding the correct scientific or chemical terms that high school seniors would understand. After a long list of theoretically precise characteristics, the author ended with a statement explaining the power of the blast **"and other godlike chemical reactions."** After all is said and done, there is still a sacred mystery about the whole concept of forgiveness: perhaps if **"and other godlike reactions"** *were added it would be easier to understand.* A mature individual in fellowship with the Divine has a capacity and an obligation to forgive and maintain friendship, fellowship, and peace with others.

Sacred writings are clear: *"Love your enemies, do good to those who hate you, pray for those who despitefully use you..."*

Forgiveness relates to understanding, tolerance, peace and goodwill among families, groups and moral citizens of the community. To be effective at the individual level, forgiveness and reconciliation require positive change in both parties. Both sides of any issue or disagreement must state their grievance and come to an agreed settlement, or confusion and conflict continues to hinder personal maturation and positive social change. Forgiveness and reconciliation go together *"hand and glove"* which suggests a relationship while working together with others for a common outcome.

Forgiveness and reconciliation are crucial relational aspects of agreement among families and the collected saints gathered for worship and fellowship. Both forgiveness and the positive results from the action have a role in confession, communion, and cohort harmony. All aspects of forgiveness lead to respect and restoration among individuals. Those who refuse to forgive or accept reconciliation disrupt the uplifting harmony of relationships and hinders the maturation of all involved. Remember, when one is disappointed by another's behavior or words, the offended one does not normally remain silent. The gossip mill starts grinding tidbits of fact mixed with misunderstanding and personal judgment. Others get involved: this unwise interference opens Pandora's Box and generates unintended consequences which makes matters worse.

12. As the consecrated, loved and select ones of God, clothe yourselves with a tender heart, kindness, humility, gentleness, and long-suffering; 13. **be generous with each other and overlook faults, forgiving all disagreements as Christ forgave you.** *14. In addition to all these put on compassionate love, which binds believers together in harmony. 15.* **And let the peace of God rule in your hearts, this will produce harmony and thankfulness** *in the assembly. 16. Allow the Word of Christ to remain in you as a treasure of wisdom; teaching and gently reminding one another in psalms and hymns and spiritual songs, singing with grace in your hearts to the Lord. 17. And whatever you do, do all in the name of the Lord Jesus, and through Him continue to give thanks to the Father. (Colossians 3:12-17 EDNT)*

Following this exposition on unity among spiritual friends, Paul expands to the home by reminding husbands and wives to demonstrate warm affection and not permit bitterness to harm their family unity or hinder their prayers. (1 Peter 3:7) After this adult behavior, Paul deals with children and parents and their interaction. Finally, the wide-range guidance for all: "*whatever you do, put your heart into it as if you were serving Christ your Master. All wrong-doing will receive punishment: and there is no partiality with God.*" (Colossians 3:23-24 EDNT)

The capacity to forgive is a targeted gift and a cherished predisposition of mature individuals who walk together in an agreed direction. This gift must be exercised regularly to maintain peace and harmony among friends and family and within a gathered faith-based group. Paul reminded young Timothy to "*fan the flame of the gift of God... For God has not given us the spirit of cowardice, but of power and of love and self-control.*" (1Timothy 1:6-7 EDNT)

For we all were once foolish, disobedient, being deceived and serving as slaves to various desires for pleasures, living in hatred and resentment, detestable ourselves, and hating each other.

(Titus 3:3 EDNT)

Introduction

"To err is human...!"

The natural man does not know the things of God, neither can they be fully identified because the spiritual light cannot shine through the darkness of the human spirit. Those who by faith receive the light are to be the illumination that penetrate this darkness to influence disobedient souls of God's mercy and forgiveness. The lost cannot see without this light and cannot hear the word of love and forgiveness unless someone interacts kindly with them and demonstrates the power of forgiveness coming through a redeemed soul. It will take God's light reflected through witnesses to convince an unbeliever that forgiveness is love and mercy from the God of Deliverance.

From the earliest records of God dealing with mankind, there has been forgiveness, freedom from unjustified accusations and promises of fairness and justice in human conflicts. In the Garden of Eden, God clothed the nakedness of Adam and Eve with animal skins establishing *"without the shedding of blood there is no forgiveness."* In accepting Abel's lamb sacrifice and rejecting Cain's bloodless garden verity, the association with the shedding of blood for forgiveness was confirmed.

Throughout the Old Testament the perpetual offering of animal sacrifices reinforced the cost of forgiveness. Then came the sacrificial death of Jesus on the Cross and the perpetual reminder through the Holy

Communion, where God constantly reminds worshipers of the necessity to forgive others.

Through Moses God initiated a plan that offenders should be presumed innocent until all the evidence was known. There are always two sides to each conflict and quick judgment by the offended or others was forbidden. Cities of Refuge were established on both sides of the Jordan River with easy access by 48 foot, straight roads always kept in repair with all obstacles removed and bridges built over natural barriers with signs clearly marked [מקלט; מקלט = **Refuge; Refuge**] with arrows at each crossroad so the offender would not be hindered in securing refuge until all the facts were reviewed. All accused were to have a fair hearing, and no one was to jump to premature conclusions without hearing the full story.

The bitterness of human nature was later expressed through Roman Law that seemed to replace the Law of God with reference to militant pursuit of an offender followed by cruel and unusual punishment. *(After all Rome did invent the curse of slow and cruel death on a cross.)* In Paul's personal struggle and conflict between the Law of God and his human nature, he wrote *"Who shall deliver me from the body of this death?"* (Romans 7:24)

It is assumed Paul was referring to the Roman practice of strapping the body of a murder victim to the back of the one accused and condemned of murder. This would cause a slow and painful death, as the decomposing body seeped poison into the body of the murderer. Paul answered his own question as he further acknowledged his human weakness and wrote, *"I thank*

God for deliverance through Jesus..." The only road out of intentional or unintentional harm to self or others is through a touch of divine grace which activates the forgiving spirit and enables all who may offend to be quickly forgiven. This is the road less traveled, but it is the shortest route to peace and harmony in all relational conflicts.

Forgiveness is not only an emotional issue – it is a reaction to human failure within ourselves and in others that brings both physical and spiritual damage to the inner spirit of both the offender and the offended. The Greek concept used in scripture for *offend* means *"cause to stumble or entice to sin."* Wrongdoing prompts one to make impromptu decisions that impacts relationships with God and others. The urgent need to express forgiveness affects the heart, the brain and the atmosphere around the situation. Delay or off-the-cuff response when one does not fully grasp the implications of all operative issues, limits prompt resolution and creates more stress. How an offence is handled determines the degree and duration of the damage caused by the wrongdoing. It also impacts the life and legacy of both the offender and the offended.

Sacred scripture provides sufficient guidance to protect individuals from being caught in the trap of retaliation. When offenses come, and they will, because the human mind is easily enticed negatively toward irrational suspicion and distrust and the human heart is quickly insulted, offended, and wounded. Civility and maturity brings people together to improve both attitude and action in relationships, but this requires forgiveness and the process of reconciliation.

The opportunity to forgive is a spiritual moment when the strength of the mind, will and emotions are confirmed so one may exercise the power of prompt forgiveness when offended or hurt by others and deal with the process of reconciliation. The power in forgiveness is divine enablement which provides individuals the capacity to examine themselves, understand the issue and correct their part of any dispute, and forgive and restore good relations with relatives, friends, and neighbors...and enemies, too!

Forgiveness is the intentional and voluntary process by which an individual undergoes a change of attitude and behavior regarding an offense and releases all negative emotions and renounces any vengefulness toward the offender. This is not the condoning or excusing of wrongdoing; it is a faith-based effort to remove any doubt about the possible cause of bad behavior by either party.

It may be impossible to restore the relationship, but forgiveness has a spiritual element that causes one to act unilaterally and not remember the offense against the transgressor and forgive themselves if there were a possibility that their attitude or behavior prompted the difficulty. The wrongdoing of others may easily stimulate bad behavior in the offended. This is part of the theology of forgiveness and requires a spark of divinity commonly expressed **"to err is human, but to forgive is divine."** Scripture is certain, if one does not forgive an offense; they become an offender before God themselves.

Human interaction and reaction to the behavior of others is not a one-way street. The offended often opens the door by attitude or action that triggers a negative response in others.

> *That is why I say, Whatever you desire, when you pray, believe that you receive it, and you will have it.* <u>*25. And when you stand up to pray, forgive anything you are holding against anyone: so that your Father in heaven may forgive you your moral wrongs.*</u> **26. But if you do not forgive, neither will your Father who is in heaven forgive your transgressions.** *(Mark 11:24-26)*

The common sense understanding of forgiveness is similar to information about an Insurance Company explaining "First Accident Forgiveness." Recently a TV ad showing a couple with one explaining an unavoidable accident and the insurance company's forgiveness program. The man was careful to provide details of the accident and that the insurance company would not hold the accident against the driver when it was not his fault. Looking at his partner, the man said, "**You see, this company doesn't hold grudges. How mature of them!**" Provided the reader internalizes this concept, they would understand the construct of forgiveness and demonstrate a degree of spiritual maturity.

Forgiveness is not just forgetting by removing awareness of the offense; it is more than pardoning or reconciliation. A genuine act of forgiveness is an effort to "*blot out the memory of the offense and behave as if it never happened.*" That is the *divine* part: to say **"I forgive"** is the easy part; to be able to treat the incident as if it had not happened requires God's assistance. This support comes through prayer and the Word and continued consecration. A little help from true friends who understand the process is a personal blessing to both parties.

> *17. Therefore if any man be in Christ, he is a new creation: observe, the old things have passed away; all things have become new. 18.* **All things are of God, who has brought us together in Himself by Jesus Christ, and has given to us the ministry of bringing people together; 19. how that God was in Christ bringing together the world to Himself, not counting their false steps and blunders against them; and has committed us to speak intelligent words that bring man and God together.** *20. Now seeing we are representatives for Christ, as though God did make His appeal through us: we implore you in Christ's stead, come together with God. (2 Corinthians 5:17-20 EDNT).*

Forgiving can become a one-way street when the offender does not acknowledge responsibility for their behavior. This means there may not be full restoration of the relationship; notwithstanding the offender's attitude, the forgiver stands free of guilt in the eyes of God. This is a good place to be!

> *9. Wherefore we devote ourselves zealously to please the Lord whether at home or absent. 10. The sum total of us must appear before the judgment seat of Christ; that the whole character of everyone may be made manifest to receive a recompense for things done in the body whether good or worthless. (2 Corinthians 5:9-10 EDNT)*

Those who fail to reconcile will retain their guilt which will fester, and eventual discipline will come from a source outside themselves. It is better for the incident to be handle only by those involved.

23. Therefore if you bring your gift to the altar, and remember that your brother has a grievance against you; 24. leave your gift before the altar, and first make peace with your brother and then return and offer your gift. 25. Come to agreement without delay with your adversary, when you have opportunity; (Matthew 5:23-24)

15. Furthermore, if your brother shall transgress, go in private and speak about his weakness: if he listens, you have gained your brother. 16. But if he will not listen, then take one or two more with you, so that each word may be confirmed by two or three witnesses. 17. And if he refuses to listen to them, tell it to an assembly: but if he refuses to listen to the assembly, let him be to you as a disbeliever... (Matthew 18:15-17 EDNT)

The process of restoring an offender is not over; once forgiveness is rejected and any hope of reconciliation is lost. Now they must be treated as an unbeliever. Concern must be maintained for their restoration and the same effort made to bring them to full forgiveness as one would work with anyone who has stumbled on the path toward heaven.

*16. Acknowledge your failures and side steps one to another, and pray for yourselves and for one another, that you may be made spiritually whole again. When a righteous man prays fervently there is great power in prayer. 17. Elijah was a man similar to us and he prayed earnestly that it should not rain, and for three years and six months no rain fell upon the earth. 18. And he prayed again, and the heaven gave rain; and the earth put forth her fruit. 19. My band of believers, if any of you do stray from the true path, and one turn you about. 20. **let the brother know, that he who turns one back from the error of his way into the right path, covers many***

faults and makes him safe, restoring his usefulness to the congregation. *(James 5:16-20 EDNT)*

Forgiveness is not only an emotional issue –it is a reaction to human failure in ourselves and others that brings both physical and spiritual damage to the inner spirit of both the offender and the offended. Wrongdoing prompts one to make a quick decision that impacts relationships with God and others. Forgiveness affects the air we breathe. Failure to fully understand the cause or implications of an offence limits forgiveness. How quickly we forgive an offense impacts ourselves and others. The Word of God provides all we should know to protect ourselves and one another for the power of being caught in the trap of retaliation when offenses come, and they will, because the human heart is easily offended. People are constantly brought together so the ministry of reconciliation can work.

1

APPROVAL and READINESS for Spiritual Growth

There are two kinds of trees in the world: *deciduous* and *coniferous*. In deciduous trees the tree remains barren during hard times. Coniferous trees have foliage that remains evergreen all year. There are minor changes, but only a close observer will notice. An evergreen tree continues to grow, making the necessary occasional changes without the distraction of dying foliage or barren branches. There is a place in God for each believer, and through mature leadership and personal discipline, a way for each individual to remain evergreen.

A green leaf signifies growth and the promise of fruit. Seeing a green leaf on a tree one instinctively knows the tree is alive. If a tree has green leaves, the evidence of life, but no fruit, the reason for life, there would be logical questions about the viability of the tree. Each individual must ask themselves: *"Will I change and become barren with the hard times or remain green, growing and productive? Will my life bear fruit? What would others say about me?"*

> *8. Finally, you must think the same thoughts, share difficulties with one another, having automatic interdependence with brotherly kindness; be tender-hearted and humble-minded: 9. you must not repay*

*injury with injury, or hard words with hard words, but bless those who curse you. For you were called to **give kind words to others and come to a well-spoken eulogy at the end**. 10. For the one wishing to love life and see prosperous days, let him avoid an evil tongue and cunning words. 11. Habitually avoid evil, and do good things; let him seek and follow peace. 12. Because the eyes of the Lord watch over the righteous, and his ears listen to their payers: but the Lord looks directly into the eyes of wrongdoers. (1 Peter 3:8-12 EDNT)*

Why should an individual or a faith-based group drift into seasons of despair and fruitlessness? Sure, there are times of preparation, renewal, correction, and growth, but this should not mean that loss of fresh and luxuriant healthiness. Paul wrote about the believer's daily renewal: **This is why we are not discouraged; although the outward nature is being worn away, the inner spirit is being refreshed with continual renewal.** (2 Corinthians 4:16 EDNT)

The EVERGREEN Devotional New Testament (EDNT) quoted in this book is a devotional rendering of New Testament Greek structured to keep believers evergreen and growing. There is a present need for daily devotional readings and individual study of the New Testament. Attending a church, with all the benefits, is not sufficient for daily growth and development of the individual believer.

Much of the value for the individual is lost in the programming for institutional advancement. Existing translations and versions of the sacred writings are so academic they have little devotional value for the reader. Thus, the EDNT is presented for the devotional use of believers to keep them ready for spiritual growth. *[www.gea-books.com]*

Spiritual growth does not take place outside of mature personal relationships. Unless all parties are supportive of each other with mature and responsible relationship that includes affection, compassion, tolerance, forgiving and spiritual commitment, there is little or no growth. There must be agreement and a natural state of readiness to provide sufficient assistance to assure a mature response to the attitude and action of others. This readiness is not approval *per se* of the actions and deeds of others but expresses an eagerness to act with enthusiasm to forgive any offense, mend any fence, and offer a steady hand to any stumbling friend. This is what makes friendship and fellowship work and creates room for personal maturity and spiritual growth.

Spiritual enthusiasm and friendship develop a mutual consent for interaction and change. Since being enthusiastic to forgive has a divine element, getting the meaning of *enthusiasm* from a secular dictionary would not tell the whole story. A dictionary may define enthusiasm as *intense and eagerly enjoyable, interest or general approval.* From a scriptural perspective, the word *enthusiasm* comes from two Greek words: "*en*" meaning *within* and "*theos*" meaning *God*. Consequently, the eagerness, speediness and inclination to forgive quickly is really the "*God within*" that provides the spiritual capacity to forgive others their wrongdoing. It suggests a spark of divinity and a God-inspired, capacity, wisdom and conviction of what is actually true about a situation and deal with it maturely.

As one continues to forgive others, they develop an ease and skill in the process. As individuals mature and follows scriptural guidance, an improved temperament, which informs personality, mood, disposition, character and outlook, is developed. The practice of forgiving *"seven times in one day or 70 times 70"* suggest a constant state of readiness to forgive. Mature individuals must have a readiness to forgive, an eagerness, and inclination to quickly forgive, without hesitation, each time there is an offense. This is a continual and persistent state of readiness to forgive, without exception. It becomes an automatic process in the life of a mature person to forgive others to maintain impartiality, personal equilibrium and a balance in all relationships.

> *14. Remind them of these things, solemnly witnessing before God not to fight with words, for they are not useful but bring destruction to the ones hearing. 15.* ***Be eager to present yourself approved to God, a workman unashamed, cutting straight the word of truth. 16. But avoid blasphemous and worthless chatter: for they will cause more disobeying of the Word. 17.*** *And their teaching will eat as does gangrene: (2 Timothy 2:14-19 EDNT)*

> *15. Look upon our Lord's long-suffering as salvation; even as our beloved brother Paul has written according to the wisdom given to him; 16. also in all his letters, when he touches on these subjects, some things are hard to be understood, things which those who lack learning and a stable foundation in the faith twist, as they do other scriptures, to their own destruction. 17.* ***For yourselves, beloved, be warned in time; do not be carried away by their impulsive errors, and. loses the firm foothold you have won; 18. but grow up in grace, and in the knowledge of our Lord and Savior***

***Jesus Chris**t. To Him be glory; now and for all eternity. Amen. 2 Peter 3:15-18 EDNT)*

1. Remind them ... 2. they are not to speak injuriously of anyone and avoid quarreling, be gentle and demonstrate a willingness to learn. 3. For we all were once foolish, disobedient, being deceived and serving as slaves to various desires for pleasures, living in hatred and resentment, detestable ourselves, and hating each other. ***4. Then the kindness and saving love of God was made manifest to all men,*** *5. it was not by personal works of righteousness that we did that saved us, but His mercy, with the cleansing power of rebirth, and restoring of the Holy Spirit; 6. which He poured out in abundance on us through Jesus Christ our Savior; 7. that being declared righteous by His grace, we should be made heirs of eternal life through faith and hopeful expectation. (Titus 3:1-7 EDNT)*

There is no God equal to your mercy, who pardons surviving warriors and forgives the wrongdoing of His people. You forgive and do not remain angry. Compassion covered our sins and forgiveness cast them into the depths of the sea. You bless us as you promised our fathers long ago.

(Micah 7:18-20 EDOT)

2

RESPECT and FORGIVENESS of Self and Others

The capacity to forgive others is a mature grace which supports the teaching of Jesus and develops within the mind, will, and emotion of individuals. It has to do with more than just obedience to scripture; it relates directly to family, friendship, and fellowship within a gathered community of mature worshipers. Automatic forgiveness, without hesitation, is the glue which holds family, friends, and a spiritual fellowship together. The "cleaving" to a marriage partner, the embracing of friendship, and the freedom and fellowship in worship all relate to the ability to forgive. Often one perceives offenses when they are not intended; in such cases the offense could be caused by the offended and should be ignored as an unforced error. The process of forgiveness is brought about by both confession and profession of faith. Transparent honesty leads to admission and confession and prepares the heart for worship and participation in sacred communion and ascribes spiritual value.

1. I exhort first of all, that petitions, prayers, intercessions, and thanksgivings, be made for all mankind; 2. for kings and all who hold high responsibilities; that we may lead a quiet and tranquil life with reverence and dignity. **3. It is good and to do**

> *this is pleasing in the sight of God our Savior; 4.*
> *who desires all men to be saved and come to the*
> *knowledge of the truth.* 5. For there is one God, and
> only one go-between God and men, the man Christ
> Jesus; 6. who sacrificed Himself to ransom freedom for
> all mankind, a witness to God's timing. 7. For this I was
> appointed a herald and an apostle, this is true, I make
> no false claims; a teacher to the nations with a message
> of faith and truth. 8. I desire therefore the men to **pray
> in every place lifting up holy hands with no anger in
> their hearts and no doubts in their minds.** (1 Timothy
> 2:1-8 EDNT)

Self-examination requires one to have a teachable spirit. In assessing a sense of personal worth one must be gentle, humble and somewhat submissive. What does respect actually mean (*"to look at and pay attention to"*) in an old unbridged dictionary? Self-respect and self-image do not come from looking into a mirror, but starts with a clear grasp of what is in the heart. There must be analysis and action to correct the observed flaws and a genuine effort to change for the better. One cannot construct the superior until the inferior has been corrected.

> *21. Wherefore put aside all moral corruption and the*
> *abundance of worthless behavior and receive with* **a**
> **teachable spirit the firmly established word, which**
> **is able to make safe that spiritual part of you that**
> **determines all behavior.** *22. You must be honest with*
> *yourselves and live by the word not merely hear it. 23.*
> *But those who listens to the word, and do not behave it,*
> *are similar to a man seeing his own face in a mirror; 24.*
> *He observes his flaws, and immediately forgets the man*
> *he saw.* (James 1:21-24 EDNT)

Respect yourself and others will respect and pay attention to you. Forgive yourself and it will be easier to forgive others. Scripture is clear *"If you do not forgive others, God will not forgive you."* Even the Prayer that Jesus taught His Disciples confirms personal forgiving as being connected to spiritual reconciliation. Behave as a human being and use the commonsense God provides and your life may still be filled with troublesome people, but a clear conscious before God is priceless.

> *36. Be compassionate, as your Father is also merciful and forgiving. 37.* **Do not pass judgment, release others from blame,** *and you shall not be condemned. (Luke 6:36-37 EDNT)*

Why do humans behave as they do? Perhaps no one really knows the answer. Before formal educators began to explain things in terms of themselves, the world was operated by common sense taught by parents and understood by children. Parents were the chief example of human deportment; that is, reasonable behavior and good manners. Children understood they were to be evenhanded, level-headed, sufficient, reliable and practical. Parents taught common sense as good behavior and sound judgment in practical matters. What my mother called "*gumption*" or "*horse sense*" a kind of "good sense" based on prudent judgment and an uncomplicated awareness or assessment of a life situation.

Parents and the extended family taught behavior, self-worth, and resourcefulness. They followed an insight similar to Dr. Benjamin Spock's often quoted wisdom, "**You know more than you think you do!** Dr. Spock seemed to suggest that common sense was the answer to reasonableness and the basic challenges of life.

It has been said that parents teach and train children to become moral citizens of society; while the extended family shows love, compassion and forgiveness. Of course, parents show love, but it is "tough love" to keep things under control. Faith-based worship and instruction attempts to make these same children mystical citizens of heaven. When longevity surpasses the ability to exchange subject matter content, parents and grandparents show strength of character, durability and patience with an extra portion of "granny love" with lots of treats and sweets. While parents have a "hands on" approach to lessons the young must learn, they often function as truant officers to keep the children in school and learning. Grandparents are more aware that their gene-pool connection is being carried on by attractive and brilliant children. And not far down the road less traveled these children will mature into representatives of the family legacy.

When grandparents see physical features; such as, eyes, nose, chin, hair, stance or the way children walk that reminds them of themselves or other family members, their attention and assessment increases for each child. It is a grand occasion to see the admiration flow to the younger generation with hopeful anticipation of accomplishments and noble achievements ahead.

Longevity turns into durability as grandparents anticipate the future accomplishments of the next generation which carries both their name, heritage and their ancestral genetic material into the future. Parents may see twenty years ahead, but grandparents see the beginning of new generations that will change the world. Yet, their experience and common sense is difficult to pass on to the children. This effort is hindered by a generation-gap which exists between them and their grandchildren. What the children see is an elderly person with a connection to their parents, who are out of touch with their generation. The accomplishments and honors earned over a lifetime are not observed or passed on to the children. A case in point:

> The event was military graveside honors for a member of the Tuskegee Airmen who flew with the 332nd fighter Group in WWII. Several high-ranking USAF Officers spoke of his wartime honors and social integration achievements (Officer Ellis earned a doctorate and had a great career after the war). Then the honoree's grandson stood and said, "I didn't know "Gramps" was famous!" How could a bright grandson not know his grandfather was a decorated Tuskegee Pilot, active in changing race relations in the military and earned a doctorate after the war? Answer: most grandparents do not talk about themselves; they are more concerned with their marvelously talented grandchildren and their future.

How does knowledge and longevity reflect on the sharing of personal history with family? It is primarily the scourge of knowledge and longevity which causes a failure to reach the next generation. When a mature person has advance knowledge of a subject, whether sacred or secular, it is difficult to present this knowledge to the young and inexperienced. As one reaches the grand status of "old age" perhaps they should review a preserved prayer from the 17th Century which appears to be current in its content. It is known as The Nun's Prayer:

> *Lord, Thou knowest better than I know myself that I am growing older and will someday be old. Keep me from the fatal habit of thinking I must say something on every subject and on every occasion. Release me from craving to straighten out everybody's affairs. Make me thoughtful but not moody: helpful but not bossy. With my vast store of wisdom, it seems a pity not to use it all but Thou knowest Lord that I want a few friends at the end.*
>
> *Keep my mind free from the recital of endless details; give me wings to get to the point. Seal my lips on my aches and pains. They are increasing and love of rehearsing them is becoming sweeter as the years go by. I dare not ask for grace enough to enjoy the tales of others' pains, but help me to endure them with patience.*
>
> *I dare not ask for improved memory, but for a growing humility and a lessening cocksureness when my memory seems to clash with the memories of others. Teach me the glorious lesson that occasionally I may be mistaken.*
>
> *Keep me reasonably sweet; I do not want to be a Saint – some of them are so hard to live with – but a sour old person is one of the crowning works of the devil. Give me the ability to see good things in unexpected places, and talents in unexpected people. And Lord, give me, the grace to tell them so.*

Perhaps this is why we see so many young ministers doing well and both young men and women teaching at the University level. They are closer to the point of learning the subject matter they wish to share. They still have a "first generation perspective" and use understandable language and examples. This gives them an edge in presentation because they remember the essential elements and building blocks that structure the subject in a simple but profound way.

As adults age and gain practical experience and more sophisticated knowledge on a subject, they are apt to present the subject skipping the essential elements and the developmental context needed for foundational learning. This does not have to be. First, if they adequately prepared their children to properly parent their own children, grandparents could limit themselves to prayers and "granny love," but if there is parental neglect or default, gramps and others need to know how to properly step into the breach and make a difference. Let us trust God to provide more good parents and grandparents. Good grandparents are desperately needed to keep the next generation on the straight and narrow way.

My grandfather Green after the death of my father, taught me many things of value. His prayers joined with Mother's prayers and became fences on both sides of the road that kept me on the straight path. Nearly a decade after my mother passed at 92, I found one of her letters where she encouraged me to pray about my life and future. Mother wrote this short prayer at the end of her letter: *"Lord, give me the sense to see my faults, not all at once, but one by one, starting with my worst, then when I have that one under control to proceed to another. Lord, erase hostilities from me so that I may approach this day in peace, not to put my faith in people but in you."* Not a bad plan for a son to follow: sometimes we have to forgive ourselves and others.

Naturally, the words of mother had great impact on me. If she had faults I could not see, then I must be unaware the of hidden faults in my own life. From the grave, the prayers of the past remain effective. Note in Luke 1:13 where the Messenger of the Lord told Zacharias, **"The prayer you no longer pray, God heard**." This elderly couple had stopped praying for a son, but God had already heard their prayer. The promised son was John, the Forerunner of Jesus. Perhaps we should have more confidence that God hears and will answers sincere prayers for our children...even without our knowledge!

Dealing primarily with the basics should be enough to participate in the upbringing of proper children when the need develops. Otherwise parents and grandparents (even the extended family) should limit their participation to prayers and "granny love" and perhaps a share more of our payers should deal with the hard lessons of life we know our children will face.

Achievements, professional accomplishments and age do not have to hinder the sharing of information with children and grandchildren. Provided it follows the K.I.S.S. formula: Keep It Short and Simple and includes the foundational steps that enabled the reaching of goals. Start at the learner's level of understanding and move them forward logically, step by step until learning becomes a happy experience.   It is not the teacher's knowledge, but the student's learning that is important.

Longevity and the age the subject matter was learned, or the experience occurred factors into the process of sharing. As a Graduate Professor, it was difficult to teach complicated data to the young and inexperienced students. They did not recall the introductory material or the essential building blocks that developed the subject. What was learned at 20 or 30 is difficult to teach at 50 or 60 to those without the basic knowledge and the essential steps which develop a particular subject.

It appears as one matures, they begin to make the false assumption that the basic facts are known, when this is not the case. Sharing subject matter presentation becomes more sophisticated by the teacher and more complicated for the learner. This is why each effort to share must start with a review of basic knowledge and the essential elements in order for the learner to grasp the scope and context of the subject regardless of the subject area.

This difficulty can clearly be seen in new editions or volumes of a textbook. For example, Earl Babbie in an early edition of *The Practice of Social Research*, provided details on how to develop an index for indirect surrogate measurement, but in a new edition simply wrote *"develop an index."* He was assuming the student knew the basic data as to how to assess facts which could not be directly measured. Why does this happen in textbooks? Publishers establish the size of a bookblock and when an author adds a paragraph or section to an existing volume, an equal amount must be omitted to make room without adding to the number of pages in the text which affects the cover and the price. This complicates the learning process for students but manages to satisfy the self-worth of the author. The writer can show advance knowledge of the subject worthy of the new edition even if it does not enhance the learning environment.

Those planning curriculum, course syllabi, and lesson plans must take into account that all sharing of subject matter must start with the basic elements of the subject and how this fits into the present situation. All learning must move from the known to the unknown. All learning is accumulative, incremental and progressive: *"precept upon precept, line upon line,"* (Isaiah 28:10-13} and at times the failure to learn a key fact may cause the failure to learn. A *precept* is a guiding principle or rule that is used to control, influence or regulate content and/or conduct. One may conceptualize a word, phrase or even a paragraph of subject matter without grasping the guiding principles or instructive elements intended as a directive for engaging the subject matter and understanding the broader implications and their relevant functional application.

Common sense is neither common nor the result of intuition. The gut-feeling called *intuition* is a sense of knowing without thought, observation or reason; however, common sense is closer to *instinct* since it is deeply-rooted and hardwired as a Divine Gift to equip the human race to fulfill both the practical and divine tasks needed to survive and replenish the earth. *(Genesis 2:7; Psalms 150:6)* Common sense is the good nature of a human being and should be practiced by all regardless of age or circumstance. (See Appendix A for more on Common Sense.)

> *3. Since His divine power has bestowed upon us all things that are necessary for true life and true worship, through the full knowledge of Him who called us to His own glory and moral uprightness: 4. since through these gifts He has bestowed upon us precious and treasured promises: you are to share the divine nature, leaving behind the corruption and passions of the world. 5. And you too have to contribute every effort on your own*

part, crowning your faith with moral excellence, and to moral excellence knowledge from books and teachers: 6. and to your knowledge self-control; and to self-control enduring steadfastness, and to enduring steadfastness godly worship; 7. and to godly worship brotherly kindness; and to brotherly kindness benevolent love. (2 Peter 1:3-7 EDNT)

1. Then Jesus said to His disciples, Crimes against moral standards will come: but serious misfortune to him through whom these crimes come! 2. It would be better for him if dead weights were placed around his neck and he was thrown into the sea, than to hurt a single little one. 3. **Give attention to yourselves: if your brother commits a moral or social injustice reprimand him; and if he apologizes, forgive him. 4. And if he commits this injustice seven times in a day, and apologizes every time, you shall forgive him.** *10.* **So likewise when you have done all those things commanded of you, say, We are unprofitable servants: we have done that which was our duty.** *(Luke 17:1-4; 10 EDNT)*

Barton, my oldest son, writing about forgiveness in *"Between the Lines and Spaces* (2009) shared his view of forgiveness:

"The word "forgive" is amazing. If you break it down, it appears to mean, "before...give." Before it is deserved, give mercy. That's what God does for us every day; He withholds judgment, and gives us grace before it is deserved. And it is never deserved. We must forgive and forget, for how can we, who have been shown so much mercy, do any less? The quicker you forgive, the better you feel. And when you forgive you create an opportunity to change the course of the receiver's life, as well as your own."

28. And one of the scribes came, and having heard the discussion, perceived that Jesus had answered admirably, asked, Which of the commandments is in first position? 29. And Jesus answered, **The chief one is,** *Hear, O Israel; The Lord your God is one Lord: 30. And thou <u>shall love the Lord your God with your whole heart, and with your whole existence, and with all your moral understanding, and with all your ability and strength</u>: 31. namely this,* **You shall love as yourself those near you. There is no other commandment greater than these.** *32. And the scribe said, Honestly, Teacher, you have truthfully said that He is One. There is none other: 33. and to love Him with all the heart, and with the bringing together of your understanding, and with all your ability and strength,* **and to love a neighbor as yourself, is more than all whole burnt offerings and sacrifices. 34.** *And when Jesus saw that he answered wisely, He said,* **You are not far from the kingdom of God.** *(Mark 12 28-34 EDNT)*

Since the fear of God is the beginning of wisdom; it follows that forgiveness is an early step toward maturity. With experience comes mellowness and reliability that assists in building relationship with others. An early assessment of the Creator was that it was not good for man to be alone; he needed a helpmate. Another element of the God's Plan was for His Creation to be "*fruitful and replenish the earth.*" The objective was to be productivity and restore what was used. A growing garden was God's schoolhouse where mankind was to learn the lesson and responsibilities of the care and cultivation of living things. The loss of the family garden was a significant hinderance to maturity. To see things grow is to recognize it is God Who causes the increase. This recognition that

God is essential to growth and forgiveness is essential to maturity.

Perhaps forgiving yourself for some misdeed that caused pain and suffering for yourself and others is harder than to forgive the shortcomings of others? Yet, mature individuals must forgive themselves as well as others. However, one often postpones action until the failure to forgive festers and causes greater difficulty.

One cannot study the Book of Beginnings without noting that "*the seed was in the fruit*" and was preserved by the moisture, pulp and the protective skin or shell for the use of mankind. The abundance of foliage and fruit were to sustain life and were to be cultivated and maintained for the survival of the human race. Human beings were to enjoy the produce of the garden and the fruit of the trees. Animals were permitted to graze on the God-given grass and foliage. Take only what was needed. Gather the seeds and replant and renew the Garden of God's provision. Yet amid this Paradise the human race began to develop a selfish spirit and a "me-attitude" that caused catastrophic failure in the responsibility to *"be fruitful, multiply and replenish"* the earth. The failure to faithfully replant the seeds created a struggle for daily food which produced fatigue and a willingness to eat the seed corn which caused a progression of struggle to feed the family. God's Will must be done God's Way!

When civilization moved from an agrarian adventure to an industrial society, many of God's early lessons were lost in the greed of the human heart. This created a materialism that dominates the existence of the whole population of the earth.

Listening to the wrong voice and going against God's Commandment caused a paradigm shift in the Garden of Eden. No longer was food to come easy from the Hand of a Benevolent God, Adam and his heirs were to toil and sweat to cultivate and generate food for themselves and their family. From the peace and pristine life of the Garden, mankind moved into the work-a-day-world to trade energy and sweat for food.

Once again God established a system to reduce greed in His supply of *manna* daily and for their Sabbath rest. Again, in the New Testament era the *"no work—no eat"*. decree went out from Paul to reestablish the *"earn your bread by the sweat of your brow."* This has not been rescinded and includes the hard work of forgiving others that is necessary to feed the spirit of harmony among family and friends.

The world has moved from a positive system to a negative structure and man quickly learns it is most difficult to move forward with a pessimistic mindset. There had to be a change of both attitude and action to have a hopeful future!

In the troubled world, each person must learn the lessons of sufficiency, productivity and forgiveness. To accomplish this one must see that God does not make junk and that each person has value, merit, usefulness, and significance. This knowledge requires one to respect the feelings and behavior of others. When the behavior of others has negative impact on associates, there must be understanding and forgiveness to maintain balance and harmony.

3

AFFECTION and TOGETHERNESS in the Family

Families are the essential building blocks of society and God's plan for growth in faith-based groups. The warmth and closeness of family life is the breeding ground for togetherness, faith-based worship and a missional lifestyle. The devotedness of friends and the tenderness of family love create a wholesome environment for growth. It is great to feel the spirit of a family atmosphere and know you belong to a family unit. Bill Gaither's lyrics about the Family of God tells the rest of the story.

The Family of God

You will notice we say "brother and sister" 'round here,
It's because we're a family and these are so near;
When one has a heartache, we all share the tears,
And rejoice in each victory in this family so dear.

From the door of an orphanage to the house of the King, No longer an outcast, a new song I sing;
From rags unto riches, from the weak to the strong,
I'm not worthy to be here, **but praise God I belong**!

I'm so glad I'm a part of the Family of God,
I've been washed in the fountain, cleansed by His blood! Joint heirs with Jesus as we travel this sod,
For I'm part of the family, The Family of God.

–Lyrics by Bill Gaither

It was good family leaders who were chosen to deal with the short comings of the early church and enabled the teaching/preaching staff to concentrate on prayer and ministry of the Word. Good believing families built good faith-based congregations with spiritual workers and moral leaders that were able to emphasize prayer and the Word. When a small boy was asked, "Which came first the chicken or the egg?" Without hesitation the answer was, *"The chicken, because God wouldn't lay an egg!"*

Applying the same logical construct to the pristine church: which came first a good church or a good family? The scriptural emphasis (Acts 6:1-15) was that good family members enabled prayer and the Word to be used to construct a firm foundation for a growing congregation of Faith. Perhaps we should think biblically and outside the box theologically about family and the church and permit this thinking to influence both individuals and families as they come together.

Love and togetherness mixed with forgiveness creates the intimacy and devotedness called family. Such closeness and informality produces love and tenderness and makes a house a home where affection and forgiveness form the bond that holds things together. The shared gender-poll of genetic material forms the superglue which bonds the children to each other. This is "family" that sticks together in good and bad times and supports the growth and development of each member as moral citizens of the community. Hopefully, they worship together in a faith-based assembly and gain spiritual knowledge to mystical citizen of heaven. With good families making good places of worship, it is a fair exchange that their children would receive sufficient guidance to become mature citizens of society. Consider the seven stones which form the foundation *for "being fruitful and replenishing the earth"* with the good seeds of faith and forgiveness.

Foundation Stone One: Concept of family introduced in Genesis 1:28 physically and theologically: be fruitful, and gain the knowledge to increase the numbers, fill and cultivate the earth. God's plan was for male and female to join together to bring new human life into the world and these siblings were to form a family. The children were to look after one another. The biblical expectation was that a family should be more a communal place of togetherness, rather than individual going their separate ways. Western culture has individualized the family, and this has influenced the church: the family altar at home and the family pew at church are gone and so are many benefits of shared faith-based worship.

Foundation Stone Two: When God saved Noah He saved his family (Genesis 6:18); when God called Abraham, He called him and his family (Genesis 12:4-5). The Abrahamic covenant (circumcision) was to be applied to all males in one's household, whether they were born into the family or were part of the household servant staff (Genesis 17:12-13). God's covenant with Abraham was familial, not individual. The family is what brings soundness, sense, sanity and common sense to public worship and a supportive society.

Foundation Stone Three: Two of the provisions in the Mosaic covenant emphasized the maintenance and cohesiveness of the family. Number 5 about honoring father and mother was meant to preserve the authority of parents in family matters and Number 7 prohibiting adultery was to protect the sanctity of marriage and construct a safe place to produce and nourish children. From these provisions flow all other Mosaic stipulations which seek to protect marriage and the family. The physical and spiritual health of the family was codified in God's covenant with Israel, but has been neglected and replaced by rules and regulations formulated by governments and institutions of society.

Foundation Stone Four: The New Testament makes similar injunctions. Jesus speaks about the sanctity of marriage and the frivolous issues that break apart the family unit. Paul described how the home should function:(a) "children, obey your parents in the Lord" and(b) parents, don't provoke your children." (Ephesians 6:1-4; Colossians 3:20-21) Also, in Acts twice on Paul's second Missionary Journey entire households were baptize at the conversion of one individual (Acts 16:11-15; 16:31-32). We know that baptism alone does not save, but one could argue that the conversion of one member of a household opens the door for the entire family to be brought to the knowledge of grace.

Even the conversion of a child can cause a whole family to repent and follow Jesus. A believing spouse can influence an unbelieving partner through lifestyle witness and influence children to follow a spiritual lifestyle. From a covenant perspective, a single member can influence the community; it is more communal than individualistic. For example, Lydia and the Philippian jailer, their household were baptized and made part of the congregation. Baptism alone does not save, since it is only by the grace of God (Ephesians 2:8-9). God's intent in the salvation of one was that the whole family would be influenced together in their attitude toward accepting God's forgiveness.

Foundation Stone Five: However, it was established by Jesus that spiritual connections were more important than blood kinship. In Luke 8:20-21, Jesus was told *"Your mother and brothers stand without, desiring to see you."* And He answered, *"My mother and My brothers are those who hear the word of God and behave it."* Then on the Cross when Jesus saw His Mother and a Disciple whom He loved (John), Jesus said, *"Woman behold your son!"* Then He said to the disciple, *"Behold your mother!* And from that hour that disciple took her to his own home. (John 19:26-27) Jesus was not saying that biological family was not important, and He was not neglecting His mother or short-changing His brothers. (His brothers were not gathered at the Cross; even though later they believed and supported kingdom work.) Jesus was saying, that in the Kingdom of Heaven the most important family connection was spiritual, not physical. This was verified in (John 1:12-13) *"But to those who welcomed Him, they were empowered to become the children of God, even to those who acknowledged His authority. These were not born by the desires of earthly parents but were born of God."* This is the Family of God for which the human family was designed to produce and restock God's family. Family members are not "tax exemptions" they are to become part of the First Family, the Family of God.

Foundation Stone Six: Scripture is clear, when one is born physically into a human family and when they are *"born again"* they are placed into a spiritual family. Using scriptural language, converts are adopted into God's family (Romans 8:15). God becomes the Father and Jesus the Brother and Believers share equal inheritance with God's Son. (Galatians 3:26-29) The physical family is the most important stone in the foundation of Society, but God's Family comes from *"every nation, tribe, people and language"* (Revelation 7:9) and is defined by *"love for one another"* (John 13:34-35) and children are an essential part of God's Plan.

Foundation Stone Seven: The purpose of both Creation and the Garden of Eden was to produce children to *"replenish the earth"* and Glorify God! A young girl was asked, *"Since the chief end of God is to glorify man and enjoy him forever, what is the chief end of man?* Without hesitation, the brilliance of an uncluttered mind responded, **"The chief end of man is to glorify God and enjoy Him forever!"** The converse of any statement is true. We may benefit from remembering and sharing this with the children.

What constitutes a family? When the Pharisees tested Jesus about the family, His response was revealing: *"Have you never read that the Creator made human beings male and female, 5. For this cause shall a man leave father and mother, and shall cleave to his wife: and the two shall become one flesh.** 6. So, it follows they are no more two, but one body (family). What God Himself has yoked together; man must not separate into parts. Jesus further explained the exceptions instituted by Moses were because the people were not "teachable."

> "v5. one flesh" is *sarx* which suggests a human body apart from the soul. Probably this is the bonding that comes with the first child and not only the emotional bonding of a couple when vows are physically consummated.

The words of Jesus make clear that those who become husband and wife must develop a *"teachable spirit."* It appears from the words of Paul each individual needs the love and assistance of others to maintain a faithful marriage. The human element always seems to mitigate against God's perfect plan and creates the need for forgiveness. The modifications of marriage are made by human beings; just as Moses tinkered with relationship problems on the Journey from Egypt to the Promise Land. The innate weakness of humanity continues to tinker and tweak the common sense that stabilizes family relationships. Forgiveness is the glue, together with spiritual dedication, that holds a family together and prepares the children for moral and ethical participation in life. The togetherness of husband and wife has built-in areas of difficulty without the interference of others. Without forgiveness the relationship crumbles.

Can two walk together except they agree the direction? Why was a man to *"leave his father and mother"* and develop a closeness with his chosen mate? It appears that parents have a different perspective on their children's marriage than the couple. The human problems of marriage are best worked out by those who are directly attached and devoted to each other without the interference and the meddling of others. Certainly, the spiritual advice and counsel of believers can be useful provided it is warm, friendly, and caring (and yes, spiritual).

It might be good for those who wish to assist a young couple in the early days of marriage or get involved only when serious trouble comes. It may be useful to review the early trial and error process of Old Testament rules for marriage.

1. Marriage is not merely a legal partnership, but a union sanctified by God. With God as a partner, marriage is endowed with a sacred and serious commitment.

2. As such marriage is not only personal but has implications for both society and faith-based groups. When one neglects the guidelines stated in scripture relative to morality and ethics, the present situation is complicated. (See Leviticus 18 for guidance with intimate relationships).

3. (Deuteronomy 24:5) Clearly advised that a newly married man should not be sent to war or given any work for one year so he could spend the first year building a relationship with his wife. This would mean the young man would have to work hard and prepare for this special first year.

4. Marriage assures the reproduction and endurance of both family and race; marriage is the foundation of the family and it logically follows that children would be born into a home with both mother and father to nurture them in the fear and admonition of God. Children should be molded into a moral citizen of the community in the process of becoming mystical citizens of Heaven.

> Note: *The Hebrew language makes clear that two becoming "one flesh" does not define the sex act; it points to the combining of two gene pools into the formation of a new body, a real person; that is a child or offspring. The Hebrew word (basar) means flesh, body, living creature, or blood relation. The Hebrew word used in Genesis 2:7 for "soul" (nephesh) was used for life in Leviticus 17:11 "The life (nephesh) of the flesh (basar) is in the blood." The word for life is the same one used for Adam becoming a " one flesh." It appears that Genesis 3:24 "Therefore shall a man leave his father and his mother, and shall cleave unto his wife: and they shall be one flesh (basar)," clearly indicates that a sexual union may produce a child.)*

5. Children must be seen as a gift from God together with momentous responsibility for parents and the larger community for their care. (Leviticus 12:) Note the procedures after childbirth. The special process with a male child were doubled with the birth of a female. Why? The female was to be a future wife and mother and special devotion must be given to the purpose of her gender in the future of the family.

6. Husband and wife must dwell together in harmony and unity. *Wives are to organize their lives around their husbands with the same respect they gave their parents. The spiritual grace of a wife can bring growth and maturity to a husband when her pure and respectful heart is observed. Such a calm and teachable spirit is priceless in God's eyes.* **This is the way holy women of ancient**

times behaved, loved and cared for their family. The scripture continues that **"husbands must be disciplined and reside together as a family, providing respectful quarters for the wife who has less strength than your own.** *The grace of eternal life belongs to you both, and your prayers must not suffer interruption.* (1 Peter 3:1-7 EDNT)

7. Family worship is essential to spiritual growth. Let each family say with Joshua *"For me and my household, we will serve the Lord."(Joshua 2:15)* We should also remind ourselves of the words of Hebrews 10:22-25:

Let us come forward with *a sincere heart crammed full of faith, having our guilty consciences purified by sprinkling, and our bodies washed with pure water: 23.* **let us not waver in acknowledging the faith we profess; we have a promise from one who is true to His word. 24. Let us keep one another in mind, always ready with love and acts of piety, 25. let us not abandon our meeting together, as some habitually do, but let us encourage one another,** *and all the more as we see the great day drawing near.* (Hebrews 10:22-25 EDNT)

7. You who are husbands must be disciplined and reside together as a family, providing respectful quarters for the wife who has less strength than your own. The grace of eternal life belongs to you both, and your prayers must not suffer interruption. (1 Peter 3:7 EDNT)

Prayer is essential to a wholesome family. At times Satan hinders prayers, but for the most part it is personal difficulties that hinder answered prayers. It has been said, "God always hears prayers and He answers, "Yes, No, or Later." Here are some reasons prayers are hindered.

(1) Immorality and money hinder marriage and the spiritual life of a family. Scripture deals with the morality issue and speaks about money.

> *4. Let marriage be held in honor among you and never let the marriage bed be defiled: but God will judge the fornicators and those who adulterate the marriage vows. 5. Let your way of life be free from the love of money; and be content with the things you have: for He said, I will never leave you, nor forsake you. 6. So we may with fluency of speech say, The Lord is my helper, and I will not fear what man can do to me. (Hebrews 13:4-5 EDNT)*

> *2. Nevertheless, to avoid immorality, let every man keep to his wife, and every woman keep to her husband. 3. Let the husband provide habitual consideration to the wife: and likewise, the wife to the husband. 4. The wife cannot claim her body as her own, but the husband: and likewise the husband cannot claim his body as his own, but the wife. 5. Do not withhold sexual intimacy from one another, except by consent for a season that you may give yourselves to prayer; and come together again, that Satan may not keep on tempting you because of irrepressible desire. (1 Corinthians 7:2-5 EDNT)*

> *7. For we brought nothing into this world, neither can we carry out anything. 8. Let us be content with food and clothing. 9. But those who are determined to be rich are tempted and caught in a trap, and into many senseless and dangerous appetites, such desires cause men to sink into present destruction and later punishment in hell. 10. For the root of all evil is the love of money: while some craving money have wandered away from the*

faith and suffered many self-inflicted and discouraging sorrows. (1Timothy 6:7-10 EDNT)

(2) A failure to forgive the shortcomings and misdeeds of another is a major problem in relationships.

Forgiveness and reconciliation are crucial aspects of agreement in any relationship. The power to forgive others for their wrongdoings is a powerful capability divinely furnished believers as a tool to assist the maturation and harmony among family, friends and associates. It was a part of the Divine Plan for maintaining peace and fellowship among believers.

> *1. Brethren, if a man should make an unintended error due to weakness, you who are regenerated, repair and adjust him with a teachable spirit; continue considering yourself, lest you also be tempted to make a false step. (Galatians 6:1)*

(3) Those who refuse to forgive and/or accept reconciliation disrupt the spiritual harmony of relationships. Anything that disrupts the fellowship of believers hinders family maturity and a current relationship with God.

> *25. And when you stand up to pray, forgive anything you are holding against anyone: so that your Father in heaven may forgive you your moral wrongs. 26. But if you do not forgive, neither will your Father who is in heaven forgive your transgressions. (Mark 11:23-26)*

(4) The failure to ask God in humble prayer within His will.

> *2. You have not, because you ask not. 3. You ask wrongly and do not receive, what you ask for is denied because you would squander it on your own pleasures. (James 4:2-3 EDNT)*

(5) Failure to value the friendship and relationship with others.

1. If there be any encouragement in Christ, if any reassurance in love, if any participation of the Spirit, if any tenderness and com-passion, 2. fill up my joy by living in harmony, having the same love, being in one accord of one mind. 3. Let nothing be done through argument or excessive pride; but in true humility let each value others more than themselves. 4. Look not after your own interests, but practice looking after the interest of others. (Philippians 2:1-11)

(6) Failure to acknowledge God in prayer mixed with faith has limited results.

6. It is impossible to please God without faith. No one reaches God's presence until he has learned to believe that God exists, and that God is one who rewards those who are seeking Him out. (Hebrews 11:6)

(7) Failure to bear one another's burdens hinders the fellowship of all concerned.

2. Practice in sharing the heavy burdens of others, and you will fulfill the principle of Christ. 3. If a man supposes himself to be something when he is really nothing, he deceives himself. 4. Let every man test himself for innocence, and then he shall rejoice in himself and not in another. 5. For every man must carry his own personal load. 6. Let him who receives instructions in the word share in support of the teacher's living. 7. Be not deceived; no man can avoid God: for whatever a man may sow this also he will reap; 8. for he who plants proceeds in the field of the material shall have a spoiled harvest; but he who plants proceeds in the field of the spiritual life shall harvest life everlasting. 9. ***And let us not become weary in doing what is right: for if we do not weaken our resolve, in due season we will***

> *collect the good harvest. 10. As we have opportunity, let us practice generosity to all, especially to those who are of the congregation of faith. (Galatians 6:2-10 EDNT)*
>
> *1. You are engaged in this by a call from Christ who suffered for us; leaving an example for us to follow His path: 22. He did no sin neither was deceit heard from His mouth. 23. Who, when abusive language was hurled at Him, used not verbal abuse; when He endured pain and distress, and uttered no threats; but committed Himself to the righteous judge: 24. on the Cross His own body took our sins, that we might depart from sins and live righteously; it was His wounds that healed you. 25. Until then you were like straying sheep, but are now brought back to the Shepherd who keeps watch over your souls. (1Peter 2:21-25}*

(8) Finally, you must think the same thoughts, share difficulties with one another, having automatic interdependence with brotherly kindness; be tender-hearted and humble-minded: 9. you must not repay injury with injury, or hard words with hard words, but bless those who curse you. For you were called to give kind words to others and come to a well-spoken eulogy at the end. 10. For the one wishing to love life and see prosperous days, let him avoid an evil tongue and cunning words. 11. Habitually avoid evil, and do good things; let him seek and follow peace. 12. Because the eyes of the Lord watch over the righteous, and his ears listen to their payers: but the Lord looks directly into the eyes of wrongdoers (1Peter 3:8-12 EDNT)

> *4. but let it be the beautification of the heart that will not fade away, even a calm and teachable spirit, which in God's eyes is priceless. 7. You who are husbands must be disciplined and reside together as a family, providing respectful quarters for the wife who has less strength than your own. The grace of eternal life belongs to you*

both, and your prayers must not suffer interruption.
(1 Peter 3: 4 and 7 EDNT)

Celebrate National Mother's Day (formerly declared by President Wilson 1914)

Emphasize Spiritual Motherhood (All believing women walking in fellowship with the Lord and young unmarrieds willing to pledge themselves to a life of moral excellence and the upbringing of children.)

18. Be careful how you listen: for those who have will be given more and those who have not shall lose what he seems to have. 19. Then came His mother and His brethren, and could not come to Him for the crowd. 20. And He was told, <u>Your mother and brothers stand without, desiring to see you.</u> 21. And He answered and said, **My mother and My brothers are those <u>who hear the word of God, and behave it.</u>** *(Luke 8:18-21)*

See the Body of Believers as THE BRIDE OF CHRIST (All Born Again Believers who are fully committed to a Spiritual Lifestyle and feel they are ready to face God in Death or Rapture.)

2. For I am zealous over you with godly suspicion: for I have joined you together with one husband that I may present you chaste and undefiled to Christ. 3. But I fear lest by any means you be deceived through cunning craftiness as the serpent totally seduced Eve, so your minds should be led astray from a singlehearted loyalty toward Christ. 4. For if a specific person well-known to you preaches another Jesus, whom we have not proclaimed, or if you receive another spirit which you have not received, or another gospel, which you have not accepted, you would do well to be patient.
(2 Corinthians.2: 2-4)

15. Look carefully how you walk, not foolishly, but in the light, 16. Buying up every opportunity, because these are *evil days. 17. Wherefore be not reckless, but prudently understand the will of the Lord. 18. Stop excessively drinking wine, which influences riotous living; more willingly be influenced by the Spirit; 19. but speak to one another in exalted verse, songs of praise, and sacred music, singing and making melody with the music of your hearts, to the Lord; 20. continue giving thanks to God the Father for all things in the name of our Lord Jesus Christ; 21. line up under one another in reverence to Christ. 22. Wives, line up under and adapt to your own husbands, as unto the Lord. 23. For the husband is in charge of the wife, even as Christ is in charge of the church: and He is the champion of the church. 24. Therefore as the church is to line up under the authority of Christ, so let the wives line up under their husbands in all things. 25. Husbands, be devoted to your wives, even as Christ is devoted to the church, and gave Himself for it; 26. that he might consecrate and purify it with the cleansing water of the word, 27. that he might present the church to himself as a glorious bride, without spot, wrinkle or blemish. 28. So must men love their wives as if they were their own body. He who loves his wife loves himself. 29. For no man ever loathed his own body; but nourishes and values it, even as the Lord values the church: 30. for we are members of his body. 31. For this reason shall a man leave his father and mother and cleave intimately to his wife, and they shall become one new body.* 32. This is a great sacred secret: but I speak concerning Christ and the church. 33. Nevertheless let each one in particular love his wife even as himself; and the wife should look to and pay attention to her husband. (Ephesians 5:15-33)*

---

*v31 A new body or "one flesh" is *sarx* which suggests a human body apart from the soul. Probably this is the bonding that comes with the first child and not only the emotional bonding of a couple when vows are physically consummated.

7. Let us be glad and rejoice and give honor to Him: for the marriage day of the Lamb has come, and His bride has made herself ready. 8. And to her was granted that she should be arrayed in fine linen, clean and white: for the fine linen is the righteousness of saints. 9. And he said to me, Write, blood-related are they who are called to the marriage supper of the Lamb. And he said to me, These are the very words of God. 1. And I saw a new heaven and a new earth: for the first heaven and the first earth were passed away; and the sea was no more. 2. And I saw the holy city, Jerusalem, coming down new out of heaven from God, adorned as a bride for her husband. (Revelation 19:7-9; 21:1-2]

Reaffirmation of Marriage Vows (Invite all married couples to reaffirm their vows and encourage all unmarried young people to affirm a life of moral excellence.) (See Appendix G)

Celebrate National Father's Day (initially announced by President Johnson 1966 and made permanent by President Nixon 1972)

Celebrate National Children's Day (Womb to 18)

A time for young women carrying a child and barren women who pray for a child to make a special dedication of themselves to "Motherhood" and pray Hannah's Prayer.

A Time to Dedicate children to the Lord.

A Time to Pray for unsaved sons and daughters.

A Time to Pray for grandchildren.

Emphasize Spiritual Brotherhood (All believing males who are committed to a missional lifestyle and cooperation with the brotherhood should be involved a "Together-Strong NETWORK". Based on James 1:27

The ancient Greeks, in whose language God gave the New Testament, discovered that if a person really cared about the circumstances of others, They might enter vicariously into that person's life experience. They called this *sympathos*, meaning "with suffering," from which comes the English word "sympathy." By means of sympathy, one enters the minds and hearts of those who struggle or suffer, to share their burdens. The early followers of Christ discovered that when sympathy was sincere, a miracle resulted among the supported. They called it *confortis*, meaning **"together strong."** and from it came the present word, «comfort.» This is the basis for the name: **"Together-Strong" NETWORK.**

(See APPENDIX C) Organize the men of the congregation into a **"Together-Strong NETWORK** to assist the ministerial leadership with the necessary services to maintain both personal and spiritual growth of the families. It is for this reason that a NETWORK has become a strategy to organize the men to participate in the work of the congregation. All men who regularly participate in the worship services, programs, and activities of the congregation are invited to become a part of the NETWORK. The men will be organized into groups or squads based on their location, shift work, trade skills and availability. The writings of James should serve as a guide to the men. In particular James 1:27:

> *Free from all that would dim the transparency in belief and conduct before God and the Father is this, to go see and relieve the orphans without a father's protection and*

the women lacking a husband in their distress, and to keep himself untainted with guilt.

Leadership will identify the needs of widows, and women alone, the sick or needy and issue a written work order. For example, a widow's roof leaks, a single mother has difficulty with raising a young son, a family needs assistance with transportation, etc. The NETWORK squad nearest the need or the one best equipped will receive the "work order" and follow-up with the assistance of others. A good orientation to "faith and deeds" is found in James 2:14-26 *14.*

What is the benefit, my cherished band of believers, if a man says he has faith, and have not deeds? Can faith save him? 15. If a brother or sister is destitute of daily necessities and has no clothing, 16. of what use is it to say to the needy, Come in and be warmed, eat all you can and depart in peace; although you give them none of the essentials which are needful to the body? 17. Even so faith without praiseworthy deeds, is like an unburied corpse left alone. 18. Yes, a man may affirm that he has faith, and not have deeds; show me faith apart from deeds, and I will show you faith by means of my deeds.

Early Christians, when they witnessed the struggle or suffering of colleagues, acted to express their common feelings with "their fellows." This is precisely why the NETWORK was established. We must build a stronger relationship with godly people who will assist with spiritual accountability to accomplish achievable things. The early believers seemed to have an understanding of mutual and parallel susceptibility to evil conditions that prevailed. As early Christians expressed their concern for one another, they created the first **together-strong network**.

This is what the men of the congregation need as an ongoing program.

[Ecclesiastes 4:10-12; Psalms 133:1; 127:3; Malachi 2:10]

Emphasize Believers as Spiritual Children of God (All believers walking in fellowship with the Lord and committed to a Christian Lifestyle.)

26. For we are all the children of God by faith in Christ Jesus. 27. For as many as have been identified with Christ by baptism have been clothed with the attributes of Christ. 28. In Christ there is neither Jew nor Greek, bond nor free, male or female; for you are all one in Christ Jesus. 29. And if you belong to Christ, then you are Abraham's offspring and Abraham's promise is your promise. (Galatians 3:26-29)

29. Let no unwholesome words come from your mouth, but only good words for enriching, that it may serve as a blessing to the hearers. 30. Never distress the Holy Spirit of God, whereby you have been marked for the day of redemption. 31. Let your bitter frame of mind, anger and violent outbreak or brawling, and abusive language, be put away from you with all hatred: 32. Become gracious to one another, tenderly affectionate, ready to forgive one another, even as God for Christ's sake forgave you. (Ephesians 4:29-32)

34. I give you a new commandment, Love one another; the same as I have loved you. 35. By loving one another, all men will recognize you as My disciples.(John 13:34-35)

4

ATTITUDE and ACTION in Missional Lifestyle

A missional lifestyle begins with a spark of faith that comes from the light of truth which brings conviction and leads to a change in behavior. It is the fresh new feeling of spring when love, faith and growth begins; it is the start of a new way of life and behavior. A missional lifestyle brings with it an *"as you go make disciples"* mindset and prompts self-worth and appropriate action to bring purpose to life and concern for others. This is where friendship, fellowship, and forgiveness enter the human equation; it is a spark of divinity that comes with conversion and creates within the human heart the capacity to forgive and live together in peace and harmony. The missional lifestyle is a perpetual springtime for the soul of a mature follower of a faith-based purpose.

The season of spring comes twice a year to the earth's atmosphere: March to June north of the equator, and from September to December south of the equator. This divide suggests that God does not take on renewal of the whole earth at once but concentrates on renewal by changing the atmosphere and environment of half the earth at a time. While part of the earth is enduring the struggles of bad weather, the other half is enjoying springtime in preparation for their trying times ahead. God even prepares the earth for correction and cure of hardships. This suggests that God's renewal is partitioned to prepare each part of the population to refresh themselves for the task of future difficulties.

Perhaps this is what evening and morning of each day was about. In the still of the night we rest to be able to face a new day. God prepares believers with the ability to forgive so they can handle future struggles. This requires personal renewal, partnership and cooperation to work together with God in changing things for the better. Positive change requires leaders and followers, thinkers and doers, faith and works, teachers and learners, parents and children, givers and receivers, individuals and groups, organizations and communities, people and buildings, projects and budgets, meetings and minutes, etc. (and you and me!)

Individuals may express their springtime in different ways. The degree of involvement may depend on location, culture, opportunity, responsibility, health and maturity; however, there are common aspects of spring that are evident in each life. As the weather warms a bit, the wind blows to clean the ground, leaves and plants start to grow and flowers appear. Spring to some may suggest love, hope, and progress, but to others it is time for *"spring cleaning"* and to make hay while the sun shines.

In spiritual terms, it is a time of new beginnings: time to celebrate Passover and/or observe Easter. Passover is a Jewish festival to memorialize God sending Moses to lead Israel to the Promise Land; Easter is associated with new beginnings and the season of Spring and for faith-based people it is the standing up again of Jesus from the grave on the First Day of Christianity. It is a time for inventory of life and time to report to the Captain of our Salvation, **"All present and accounted for, Sir!"** A military unit may be declare "Combat Ready" not because of battle experience, but because of knowledge, training, and mindset. In practical terms springtime translated into "spring cleaning" of home and hearth as well as "mind and heart" to create a fresh start.

Springtime brings green leaves; they are the evidence of life and the promise of fruit. Individuals must not only present themselves humbly confessing sin and accepting the grace of forgiveness, they must show evidence of life by continually bearing fruit. It is a time for action, **"All hands-on deck! Battle stations --this is not a drill!"** This means: each person must step into their rightful place, know and exercise their role, and function properly under the circumstances. Just as the military cross-trains individuals to take up a fallen comrade's assignment, families must prepare each individual to step into the beach when one is away. A mother become both father and mother; a sister becomes a surrogate mother; a brother helps guide a younger child. The absence of one may cause extra work by others, but the family spirit must continue.

Nothing but leaves is a failure to produce fruit. This kind of life is disappointing to Jesus. When one thinks about the sacrifice of Jesus to bring salvation to mankind, it becomes clear that a life with leaves only and no fruit does not demonstrate the change which a redemptive spring brings to life. Without fruit, there are not seeds and no future generations to follow God's Garden of Eden Edict **"Be fruitful and multiply and replenish the earth!"**

*12. And on the next day, when they left Bethany, Jesus was hungry: 13.and seeing in the distance a fig tree with leaves, He went to find fruit: and when He came to it, **He found nothing but leaves**; for the season for figs had not come. 14. And Jesus spoke to the tree, No man will ever eat fruit from you again. And His disciples heard it. (Mark 11:12-14 EDNT)*

> Let love and faithfulness never leave you; bind them around your neck, write them on tablets. Then you will win favor and a good name in the sight of God and man. Trust in the LORD with all your heart and lean not on your own understanding: in all your ways submit to Him, and He will make your paths straight. Do not be wise in your own eyes, fear the LORD and shun evil. This will bring health to your body and nourishment to your bones.

(Paraphrase of Proverbs 3:3-6)

Missional behavior is adopting the thinking, action, and practices of a missionary in order to globalize the message of mercy, grace and forgiveness. Missional living is working together with God in advancing the message of redemptive grace to the world. Wisdom brings authenticity and genuineness to the daily lives of those seeking to change the world around them. In Psalm 8: 32-35 wisdom speaks further to the faithful who attend with interest to instruction and are blessed by keeping to the proper pathway. There is a war: those lessons are on the final test.

Attitude is a predisposition or mindset, outlook and behavior in a given situation. Action or behavior is the result of this attitude. At times it gives one boldness and fluency of speech at other times the same person may be reasonably quite or totally angry. This is where self-control enters behavior, especially in a missional mindset. It takes special commitment on the part of individuals, families, groups, communities, and organizations to adopt their thinking, practices and behaviors to that of a missionary in order to advance the gospel and faith-based living. Missional behavior is working together with God to advance His agenda.

> *25. But whosoever bows down to observe the complete prescriptive usage and the unrestrained opportunity to continue in the word and not become a forgetful hearer, but one who behaves the prescribed deeds,* **this man shall by the blood be set apart for consecrated action***. 26. If any man among you seem to be devout, and restrains not his unnatural language, he deceives his own heart and his service to God is ineffective. 27.* **Free from all that would dim the transparency in belief and conduct before God and the Father is this, to go see and relieve the orphans without a father's protection and the women lacking a husband in their distress, and to keep himself untainted with guilt.** *(James 1:25-27 EDNT)*

Action is engagement that leads to achievement and accomplishment. Jesus is the ultimate example of missional action explained in Philippians. Note also the words of Jesus in the Gospel of John:

> *1. If there be any encouragement in Christ, if any reassurance in love, if any participation of the Spirit, if any tenderness and compassion,*
>
> *2. fill up my joy* **by living in harmony, having the same love, being in one accord of one mind. 3. Let nothing be done through argument or excessive pride; but in true humility let each value others more than**

> *themselves. 4. Look not after your own Interests, but practice looking after the interest of others. 5. Let your disposition and thoughts be the same as Christ Jesus:* 6. although having a divine nature, did not cling to His equality with God: 7. but stripped Himself of His rightful divinity, and took upon Himself the nature of a servant, and was made in the likeness of men: 8. and appearing in human form, He humbled Himself, and became obedient even to death on the cross. (Philippians 2:1-7 EDNT)

> 15. I no longer call you (servants) or bond-slaves; because a bond-slave does not know what his Lord does: **but you I have called friends; for all things that I have heard of my Father I have made known to you.** 16. You have not chosen me, but I have chosen you, and **appointed you to go out and bring in fruit, and that your fruit should remain:** and that <u>you should obtain answers to your prayers to make them fruitful.</u> 17. These things I command you, so that you may love one another. (John 15:15-17 EDNT)

Paul's life after conversion established a pattern for a missional lifestyle. He left his comfort zone, became self-employed as a tent-maker to support his ministry and those working with him in his travel to foreign places to reach new converts, follow-up conversion, discipleship training for future leaders and establishing new congregations. His own writings recorded in scripture tells the story of his life and missionary work as he reached out to the Gentiles with the message of grace and inclusion.

> 11. For the saving mercy of God has appeared to all mankind, 12. instructing us to deny all wickedness and worldly desires and to now live discreet, honest, and God-fearing lives in the world. 13. Looking for the blood purchased hope, and the magnificent appearing of the great God and our Savior Jesus Christ; 14. Who gave Himself for us, that He might ransom us from

all wickedness, and purify a people as his personal treasure*, eager for good deeds. 15. Speak encouraging words about these things and admonish with authority. Let no man look down on you. (Titus 2:11-15 EDNT)

---

* v14 The Greek word used for possession was *"perosseous""* from the *present participle feminine* of a compound [peri] and [eimi] meaning "being beyond usual, i.e. special (one's own). Yet the KJB translators chose to use the word "peculiar" from the Latin [peculium] meaning one's own property or in Roman law meaning "private property". Although it did not essentially change the meaning for English readers because "peculiar" was common in 1611, but this translation became a problem later as some individuals used the concept of "being peculiar" as a standard for holiness instead of a clean heart.

A missional reality supports a lifestyle that coalesces around a personalized grasp of scripture that offers a faith-based direction, a sociological shift, and distinct behavior to extend witnessing through missional behavior. The missional mindset is placed in the context of viewing the Cross through the Empty Tomb, seeing culture as a vehicle of communication, a faith-based group as a force to work with not of a field in which to work, because each community of the world is a mission field ready for harvest. Paul's ministry was the challenge of the city square and/or the market place. He cast a broad net in his travels and was all things to all people in an effort to win some. Sadly, the workers are few! Believers pray for missions but produce little action that would change people or mitigate the cause of present difficulties.

Traveling opens many doors for the gospel. The real challenge for a faith-based lifestyle is in the marketplace, out where the people are daily. At a New York airport waiting in line for a delayed night flight, two gentlemen were in line talking around me. When they would not break line, their conversation was forced on me. Understanding their frustration, my Delta Flying Colonel Card was used to take them to a more private place to wait. The Crown Room was almost deserted. Soft drinks were in the refrigerator and little fish crackers on the counter, so the munching began.

After a while, one asked, *"Do you work for the airline?"* A negative answer was not sufficient, the follow up question dealt with my occupation. They were told about my travels, writing and speaking. One asked, *"What do you write?"* Sharing with them about discipleship, evangelism and dying churches, one said, *"My church is spiritually dead, and I am too!"* With this the other one decided to leave. Alone, God worked His mysterious process of renewal and commitment. At appears that God separates the sheep and the goats and the tares from the wheat. When God opens the door, believers must focus on the task at hand.

A note on Delta stationary from the Crown Room arrived in the mail. It listed *"Seven things God did for me today."* Spiritual outreach is not dead; the cause of Christ is alive and well; it is just functioning better on an individual basis than it is at the institutional level. Why is this happening? Faith-based leaders and parents have failed to develop a culture and lifestyle that includes the practice of personal witness to God's saving grace.

Local congregations must seek to enhance the quality of daily lifestyle involvement by individuals rather than the quantity of attendance at scheduled service. Places of education must do more that deal with facts; faith must be integrated into learning to make a significant difference. Spiritual change in people or conditions of society may not be altered by prayer alone, because prayer does not change *"things"* it changes *"people, and people changes things!"* This is a syllogism *"a deductive scheme in a formal argument consisting of a major and a minor premise and a conclusion."* The original syllogism has been changed or misquoted as *"Prayer changes Things."* Usually, a short-cut is not the route to progress. God said, "Redeem the time." This is a process of saving time and working efficiently and effectively without waste or loss. The original syllogism was constructed:

DEDUCTIVE ARGUMENT
"People cause things"

Major Premise
Whereas: *Things need to be changed*
Minor Premise
Whereas: *Prayer has power to change people*
Deductive Scheme
Whereas: *People cause things;*
Whereas: *Things need to be changed;*
Whereas: *Prayer changes people*
Conclusion
Therefore: *Prayer changes People and People change Things.*

Since people rather than circumstance are usually the instigator of things which cause problems, praying about circumstance or things is not the process established in the Word. Prayer is important, but it must be personal, specific, and focused particularly on the human element and not on circumstances or the condition. Prayer changes people and people change things, is a missional mindset which always does more that is required in the realm of spiritual activity, especially in the areas of outreach and forgiveness.

Spiritual behavior causes one to seek the source of the pain. Where did it originate? Did my behavior cause this difficulty? Am I partially to blame for the situation? Was the situation misunderstood? Was the response reasonable? Do I need to forgive myself or someone else? Find out where the pain is originating, do not just try to make it go away. Forgiveness allows the offender to change for the better. Choices are what make life what it is - stop blaming Satan or *"doing nothing."* James discussed this matter in two parts: one for the believer who is tested (vs.12,13); the other for the offender who acts improperly (vs.14,15):

Part One:

12. Blood-related* and fortunate is the man who flinches not under the enticement of testing: for when he is proved trustworthy, he shall be given the wreath of honor that verifies vitality, which God promised to all who worship out of a benevolent heart. 13. Let no man say when he is enticed, God allured me to evil: for God does not use wickedness to validate the trustworthiness of any man. (James 1:12,14)

---

* v12 To bless, in Middle English used at the time of KJV, had a meaning related to "blood" used to consecrate an altar; thus, the use of "blood-related."

Part Two:

14. But every man is attracted to wicked deeds, when he chooses action based on personal desire, and hope of pleasure. 15. Then when personal desire has joined together with enticement, it produces a voluntary transgression: and this offense produces separation from observant morality, and at the end separation from God. (James 1:14-15)

Delay may mean a negative reacting to an personal obligation. Since opportunity equals obligation, and there is no responsibility without accountability: one must always correct the inferior before attempting to construct a superior.

9. Wherefore we devote ourselves zealously to please the Lord whether at home or absent. 10. The sum total of us must appear before the judgment seat of Christ; that the whole character of everyone may be made manifest to receive a recompense for things done in the body whether good or worthless. (2 Corinthians 5:9-10 EDNT)

What does a missionary know and how do they feel about the lost world? Beyond a doubt they have been called to serve outside their comfort zone and must leave some family and friends and travel into a strange land. Confronted with new language and culture, they take courage. Called and appointed Missionaries know they must live a life worthy of financial and prayerful support from an extended constituency. Aware of limited resources and through fund raising, they must replace what is spent, or their work cannot continue. They are conscious of a budget of time and money. A missionary family has a totally different perspective on money matters and time use, than a state side family. A missionary family lives a different life.

A family involved in missions, cultivates a positive mindset that God is in charge of their lives and their work is a spiritual mission. Missionaries teach their children to live on a limited budget and that every cent saved enhances their chance of winning a soul for Christ. In fact, the missionary lifestyle is often lonely and full of daily difficulties. Without safe living quarters, clean bed sheets, good food on the table, and with only local natives protecting them against hostile forces, missionary families develop an uncertain way of life. Can we say, *"God bless the missionaries!"* Then in the next breath say, *"Lord help me to walk the right pathway and demonstrate a missional lifestyle to others and be supportive of those called to serve oversea while I am permitted the security of home, family, friends in the USA".*

James wrote about a pure an unadulterated lifestyle that acted with a missionary perspective. Sanctified eyes that could see each child without the influence of a believing father as needing surrogate nurturing. They could observe women alone who lack a husband in their hardship or misfortune that needed support and care from an extended family. In addition to doing good for orphans and women alone, those with a missional lifestyle endeavor to extend their outreach through each opportunity in each observable circumstance.

> *19. Wherefore, my cherished band of believers, let everyone be ready listeners, slow to express our mind, slow to take offence: 20. for the anger does not bear fruit acceptable to God. 21. Wherefore put aside all moral corruption and the abundance of worthless behavior and receive with a teachable spirit the firmly established*

word, which is able to make safe that spiritual part of you that determines all behavior. 22. You must be honest with yourselves and live by the word not merely hear it. 23. But those who listens to the word, and do not behave it, are similar to a man seeing his own face in a mirror; 24. He observes his flaws, and immediately forgets the man he saw. 25. But whosoever bows down to observe the complete prescriptive usage and the unrestrained opportunity to continue in the word and not become a forgetful hearer, but one who behaves the prescribed deeds, this man shall by the blood be set apart for consecrated action. 26. If any man among you seem to be devout, and restrains not his unnatural language, he deceives his own heart and his service to God is ineffective. 27. Free from all that would dim the transparency in belief and conduct before God and the Father is this, to go see and relieve the orphans without a father's protection and the women lacking a husband in their distress, and to keep himself untainted with guilt. (James 1:19-27 EDNT)

True evangelism is meeting the needs of hurting individuals and families at the earliest point in time at the farthest distance from the place of worship. Thinking the way a missionary normally does causes one to see opportunities where others simply see troubles and trials. In the presence of family disfunction and personal difficulties there are opportunities to lead others into the House of God for vertical soul cure and horizontal fellowship. This can truly be *"snatching souls"* from the hands of Satan and bring them into the Arms of God.

27. Free from all that would dim the transparency in belief and conduct before God and the Father is this, to go see and relieve the orphans without a father's protection and the women lacking a husband in their distress, and to keep himself untainted by the world. (James 1:27 EDNT)

What is missing in many faith-based groups is an organized class structure designed both to teach Bible content and special textbook courses on subjects of interest to the people. There are few "Antioch-type Teaching" efforts similar to Saul and Barnabas who for *"one whole year"* (365 days) taught converts before the public saw the converts as disciples becoming faith-based learners (Acts 11:19-30). At Antioch it was the secular merchants who recognized that these disciples *"transacted their business in a Messiah-like manner."* There must be systematic teaching for new converts and structured guidance for discipleship. There are few lessons on family life, family budget, raising children, spiritual outreach to the community; there is little or no scheduled community and family involvement in the process family life or faith-based education.

Local leaders should remember that in Acts 11, it took Saul and Barnabas *"one whole year"* daily teaching converts before their lifestyle was recognized by a secular community. That was 365 days; not just an hour a week. A study group requires a learning leader, a teacher/coach/mentor to provide guidance for an informed discussion. Individuals in class structure must do advance study to become an informed participant to create a learning environment required for individuals. This creates collective growth and lifestyle recognized by the public.

Understanding and following the classic principles of teaching will enhance the learning experience. The end is worth the journey, but some are not willing to walk the pathway that prepares them for biblical instruction less it reflect on their personal lifestyle. Preparing to teach requires patience, prayer, persistence, concentration, and serious study. All who prepare to teach must find a quiet and restful place to study.

During World War II in a Luftwaffe Prison Camp in England that consisted only of German airmen, a modern exponential explosion of social change occurred. From the testimony of a Medical Doctor present, a group of British women decided an act of Christian charity would be to share their bread ration with the German POW's. When half-loafs of bread were placed on the table, the German ranking officer complained to Dr. A. E. Wilder-Smith about the half rations. When he was told about the women sharing their bread ration, it opened his heart to Dr. Wilder-Smith's witness of God's mercy and grace. It is a record of exponential change where most of the German inmates of the camp embraced a faith-based change in their life. It is believed that acts of kindness in lifestyle witness can enlarge the hearts of the hardest of men. Perhaps the assembly celebration should produce a daily lifestyle witness that could be expressed as the sweet bread of life sacrificially shared. Shared daily bread was like CAKE –Christian Acts of Kindness Each-day.

The *missional* construct rediscovers the true identity of *"those belonging to the Lord"* as spiritual witnesses to the world and understands the final words of Jesus to His followers, as a Lifestyle Challenge to Believers rather than a program for an organized house of worship. In the scripture below please notice that Jesus was speaking directly to His followers about **His authority and power and sharing what He expected in their future lifestyle,** *"as you go make disciples of all nations"* reminding **them to identify future disciples with the work of the Godhead**: the Father is the Forgiver; the Son is the Savior; the Holy Spirit is the Comforter, Enlightener, and *Paraclete* (called to assist and encourage) enabling believers to live a missional lifestyle and realize that the end is worth the spiritual journey. Those who accept the scriptural change that comes with conversion, must be taught all that Jesus began to do and teach. When this is accomplished the convert realizes that the Presence of Jesus is with them continually as long as a faith-based lifestyle is daily practiced.

5

PEACE and HARMONY during the Collect

At times, traditions and old customs should be retained; they come from an unhurried time in history when people took service to God and others seriously. There was a time when the chosen leader sensed the needs of a group and prayed for those present at the beginning of a service. This was a common-sense prayer based on the needs of the people discerned by the leader and agreed to by the congregants. As the leader prayed, the people gave consent to the prayer and agreed with the judgment of the leader. It was a collective agreement; a kind of one mind, one accord, in one place. With emphasis on the first syllable, it was called the *col′lect.*

In the pristine church, before materialism took over the world, the term *col′lect* meant *the gathering of the people together and was associated with a general opening prayer by the leadership to enable the gathered group to approach the meeting with a clear conscious in agreement as to their common needs.*

The leader prayed a general prayer and identified the discerned needs of the people and they agreed with a confessional "Amen!" The *collect* was to bring conviction or agreement with the verdict as to the shortcomings of the people. Honest confession then preceded song, worship and praise for the value of Divine influence in the circumstance of each life.

Goodwill and freedom from strife were part of the peace and harmony God ordained and the pristine church practiced and is now expected by the gathered ones. Tragically, the original construct of the *"collect"* has been corrupted and reduced to a "collection plate" for the church budget. A gathering of funds and the accountability for the use of funds often disrupt the peace and harmony of congregants. Provided sacred writings are maturely noted, the faithful will generously support the financial needs of their place of worship. An old adage remains true, **"Where God guides, He provides!"** Yet, money is allowed to disrupt the prayer, worship, peace and harmony of many faith-based operations.

3. Since His divine power has bestowed upon us all things that are necessary for true life and true worship, through the full knowledge of Him who called us to His own glory and moral uprightness: 4. since through these gifts He has bestowed upon us precious and treasured promises: you are to share the divine nature, leaving behind the corruption and passions of the world. 5. And you too have to contribute every effort on your own part, crowning your faith with moral excellence, and to moral excellence knowledge from books and teachers:

> *6. and to your knowledge, self-control; and to self-control enduring steadfastness, and to enduring steadfastness godly worship; 7. and to godly worship brotherly kindness; and to brotherly kindness benevolent love.*

(2 Peter 1:3-7 EDNT)

The rulers of the world struggle to get peace with a mindset: *"We will have peace if we have to fight for it."* On the other hand, faith-based individuals and groups have a sense of peace and harmony, but have to struggle to keep it operative in the area of faith and family. To maintain accountability, each individual must accept responsibility for maintaining a moral and ethical relationship with others. The obstructions that block the road less traveled occurs when those responsible fail to take immediate action to restore transparency and integrity to the fellowship through forgiveness and reconciliation.

> *9. God is faithful, by Whom you were called into the fellowship of His Son Jesus Christ our Lord.* 10. **Now I encourage you, brethren, by the name of our Lord Jesus Christ, that you all speak the same thing unto reconciliation and that there be no divisions among you; but that you be joined together in harmony and intentions with the same mind and with the same conclusion.** *(1 Corinthians 1:9-10 EDNT)*

A condition of leadership in the pristine church was clear: leadership must not be greedy for *"filthy lucre."* In many cases, the congregation has not been well-served and has been short-changed by materialistic and selfish leadership. It is of interest that the New Testament uses the term *"filthy lucre"* to indicate money or ill gained profit, and refers four of the five places to the income of leaders. This suggested that those in faith-based positions were susceptible to the debilitating influences of money. Sadly, this trend continues to the shame of many benevolent and humanitarian groups.

When leaders fail to understand the collective needs of the people and that morality should have priority over money, there will be no instruction for the constituency in unselfish economics and the acquisition and use of personal wealth. How can there be teaching with enthusiasm about *"money matters,"* when leaders either do not understand or refuse to follow known ethical guidelines? The teaching of *"gold, glory and glamour"* and false materialistic prosperity has crippled many faith and/or public-spirited operations. This speaks loud and clear that guiding principles are being violated and suggests the need for the restoration of moral leadership as a starting place to remove anything that could disrupt the harmony and balance of integrity and reliability among humanitarian groups.

No one should begrudge adequate support for faith-based and/or moral leadership,* but to gather and store financial resources for personal use rather than the advancement of the benevolent objectives is wickedness (iniquity) or *"immoral and grossly unfair behavior."* *"Do not muzzle the ox that treads out the corn"* (1 Corinthians 9:9) means workers should have a living wage not a super abundance of wealth at the expense of people trying to support a compassionate and ethical public service. Leaders are not chosen to become rich, but to advance a principled cause. Being religious is not enough! Violation of ethical guidance can weaken or even negate the positional influence of good leaders with a capacity to provide and expand public service. [See Matthew 7:21-23; Luke 13:25-28]

---

*1 Timothy 5:17 is clear that Paul. as a bi-vocational minister used his "tentmaking skills" to support himself and his ministry group, wrote to young Timothy that those who labored in the Word and teaching were worthy of double honor "respect and remuneration," but this did not include overly generous wages beyond the capacity of those being served or the ongoing needs of the poor and neglected.

When individuals collective gather for cooperative service and offer themselves, their talents and energy for a worthy cause, there must be freedom from strife and disagreement. Should anyone know a fellow participant had a grievance against them, sacred writings and ethics are clear, to advance personal fellowship and the group purpose and mission there must be an effort to reconcile with the offended one. A known need for reconciliation must be acted upon without delay or excuse. Ethical guidance instructs one to resolve the issue before continuing their participation. Perhaps, this is why in faith-based worship each offering is immediately prayed over and sanctified for the intended use.

Gifts are measured by intent and the cost to the giver. The Divine assignment of *"spiritual equity"* is based on these considerations. This is why all gifts and offerings must be sanctified by prayer to cleanse "filthy lucre" from less than genuine motives of the giver. Note two references: the widow's mite, the smallest of Roman coins, was judged as *"more than the gifts of the rich."* (Mark 12:41-44; Luke 21:11-4) The widow's mites the Greek *lepta* -- two coins worth about 6 minutes of an average daily wage in Judea. Yet, her gift was evaluated as worth more than the coinage value of gifts by the rich. On another occasion when a man tried to buy spiritual authority he was told *"Your money will perish with you unless you repent."* (Acts 8:20-22) Gifts to advance a worthy cause are sanctified prayer and God adds or denies spiritual equity, not on the coinage value, but each gift is assigned an equity value based on the intent and cost to the giver.

> *Your money disappear with you, because you thought the gift of God could be purchased with money. 21. You have no part or share in this ministry: for your heart is not right with God. 22. Repent of your wrong doings and pray, if perhaps the thought of your heart may be forgiven.* (Acts 8:20-22 EDNT)

> *6. Remember the saying, he who sows in a miserly manner shall reap miserly; and he who sows generously shall reap an abundant harvest. 7. Let every man give as he purposed in his heart; not reluctantly or under constraint: for God loves a prompt and willing giver. 8.* ***Now God is continually able to overflow you with self-sufficiency always making you competent to pour out to the good of others:*** *9. as it is written, His generosity is scattered to the poor; His love-deeds are never forgotten. 10. Now He who supplies plenty of seed for the planting also furnishes bread for your table, and multiplies the seed sown and increases the fruit of your benevolence; 11. your being enriched unto all liberality causes us to give thanks to God. 12. The rendering of this benevolence not only supplies the needs of the saints, but causes a wealth of thanksgiving to God; 13. by evidence of this service they glorify God for your conviction and response to the gospel of Christ and for your liberality in sharing with others; 14. and by their intercession for you their earnest desire goes out to you to surpass your grace and generosity. 15. Thanks to God for His indescribable generosity to you.*

> (2 Corinthians 9:6-15 EDNT)

It appears that God looks seriously at any break in morality and ethics as well as fellowship and funding of worthy causes. (Hebrews 10:21-25) The blessings of participation in service to God and man are diminished by intent and attitude.

> *21. Since we have a high priest over the house of God; 22. let us come forward with a sincere heart crammed full of faith, having our guilty consciences purified by sprinkling, and our bodies washed with pure water: 23. let us not waver in acknowledging the faith we profess; we have a promise from one who is true to His word. 24. Let us keep one another in mind, always ready with love and acts of piety, 25. let us not abandon our meeting together, as some habitually do, but let us encourage one another, and all the more as we see the great day drawing near.* (Hebrews 10:21-25 EDNT)

From a faith-based perspective, believers are to be of one mind and in one accord gathered in one place to best receive the blessings of God. Certainly, individuals may be blessed in the stillness of private devotion, but there are advantages of being gathered as believers for collect, confession, communion, worship, fellowship and service. Although personal and private devotions are vital to moral and ethical living, each opportunity to serve God and mankind equals a clear obligation. The acknowledgment of the value of God in all aspects of life should not be forsaken or hindered by improper behavior.

Solidarity and unity are important aspects of faith-based living, because worship is the vertical expression to show the *worth and value* of God in all aspects of life.

Worship is more than a time of fellowship and sharing with others; worship must be a time of personal prayer and warm exaltation of the value of God in life and death. Worship must be preceded by confession and accompanied by communion and group fellowship, but personal devotion is the focus of a faith-based lifestyle. True reverence is a vertical experience which brings peace, goodwill, and reunion with God and reconciliation with others.

6

PRAYER and RENUNCIATION in Confession

The prayer of confession and the abandonment of wrongdoing are essential steps in relieving guilt and a prerequisite to participation in true worship and communion with God. A person may stumble and make an unintended error, but a mature individual does not intentionally "*practice wrongdoing*" or continue to repeat offences. Bad behavior must be acknowledged and forgiveness requested with the intent not to repeat the same mistake ... *so help me God!* Wrongdoings that are not forgiven will cause the weight of guilt to entangle one in a host of shortcomings. All that does not measure up to the standards of mature adult behavior must be acknowledged and abandoned prior to reconciliation or any attempt to participate in true devotion to a Higher Power.

> *1. Therefore, since we are watched from above by such a cloud of witnesses, let us rid ourselves of all that weighs us down, and the sin that so persistently surrounds us, and let us run with steadfast endurance, the course that is marked out before us, 2. let this fix your eyes on Jesus the origin and the crown of all faith, who, to win His prize of blessedness, endured the cross and made light of its shame, Jesus, who now sits on the right of God's throne.* (Hebrews 12:1-3 EDNT)

All mature individuals must qualify their mind and heart for valuing God in worship. Singing hymns and listening to others pray is not sufficient to prepare the heart for true devotion. Sin separates one from God and personal confession or admission of culpability must be forthcoming in the preparation for all religious observance to show the worth and value of God in all of life. The relationship with God must be kept current and fresh through confession, obedience and the gathering together for prayer and genuine fellowship. There must be no pretense, superficial or impulsive behavior. God's House is the "House of Prayer" not a den of thieves and cut throats. In the past the church was a gathering of family and friends, but some have made a religious service a meeting of strangers. This further complicates the areas of concern in relationship and fellowship.

One must prepare both mind and heart for participation in worship. A casual approach to worship is sacrilege, a violation of spiritual decorum, irreverent and disrespectful of the sacred. Worship is not the time and place to *"get your heart and mind fixed;"* this should be done as advance preparation for true worship. Some eight (8) decades ago in 1936, when church was still worship instead of entertainment, James E. Orr using Psalm139:23-24 wrote timeless lyrics about preparing for worship.

> **Search me, O God, and know my heart today,**
> *Try me, O Savior, know my thoughts, I pray;*
> *See if there be some wicked way in me;*
> *Cleanse me from every sin, and set me free.*
>
> *I praise Thee, Lord, for cleansing me from sin;*
> *Fulfill Thy word and make me pure within;*

Fill me with fire, where once I burned with shame;
Grant my desire to magnify Thy name.

Lord, take my life, and make it wholly Thine;
Fill my poor heart with Thy great love divine;
Take all my will, my passion, self and pride;
I now surrender, Lord, in me abide.

When one does not acknowledge personal guilt in a relationship gone bad, their trouble is just beginning. Confession is part of remaining current with God and others. The life of a believer is consistently in harmony with God's Word and His will. Confession and renunciation of all behavior that does not please God is required to remain current and walk in fellowship with God and man.

When Paul was guiding Roman believers in their spiritual walk, he was careful to share that their relationship was without pretense and was to be a life of both affection and attachment to others. In Romans 12:9-21, Paul provided a formula for living an overcoming life and maintaining relationships.

9. Let love be without hypocrisy. Hate what is wrong. Cleave to the good. 10. Have tender affection for the believers; go before one another as an honorable guide; 11. do not delay your enthusiasm; be on fire in the spirit; serving the Lord as a slave; 12. rejoice in hope; remain steadfast in time of trouble; be persistent in the habit of prayer; 13. contribute your share with reference to the needs of the saints; give attention to hospitality. 14. Bless all who persecute you: bless and curse not. 15. Share the happiness of those who rejoice, and share the sorrow of those who are sad. 16. Maintain harmony with one another. Set your mind on high things, but accept humble ways. Do not think too highly of yourself.

17. Never pay back injury for injury. Aim to do what is honorable in the sight of all men. 18. As much as you can, live peaceable with all men. 19. Never avenge yourselves dearly beloved, but leave room for Gods anger: for it is written, Vengeance is mine; I will repay, said the Lord. 20. There is another test, if your enemy hunger, feed him; if he thirsts, give him drink: for in so doing you will make him feel a burning sense of shame. 21. Never permit evil to conquer you, but get the better of evil by doing good. (Romans 12:9-21EDNT)

There is a dichotomy in human relationships: somethings are totally "I" and other things and completely "We." This is not a contradiction; it is the reality of life and must be constantly considered to be operative. When one makes a "we- issue," when in reality it is an "I-issue," and *vice versa*, real difficulty in relationships occur. When an individual takes credit for a group achievement, there will be hard feelings. If an individual involves others in a matter that should remain private, conflict will happen. If there were disagreement or disfunction within the relationship of two individuals and an extra person attempts to reconcile these differences without understanding the situation, sparks fly and harsh words are spoken.

Personal, interpersonal, and intrapersonal relationships are all difficult to manage. This is where maturity, wisdom, and a spiritual dimension enters relationships. This brings understanding to an individual's need to forgive and the requirement of agreement by both parties to bring about reconciliation. Forgiving is in the "I" realm and reconciliation is a "We-event."

When one does not forgive, God does not forgive! Facts from scripture makes clear that *God will hold an* *unforgiving individual accountable for the things they fail to forgive in others; their unforgiving spirit makes them guilty of the same offenses for which they are not willing to forgive.* The failure to acknowledge wrongdoing is the problem. Often the offense is words* rather than deeds and the old saying *"Sticks and stones may break my bones, but words will never hurt me!"* is simply not true. James acknowledges the mighty power of the tongue. He associates the language produced by the tongue as being responsible for *"a whole world of w wickedness."*

---

*(James 3:1-12) clearly states the power of the tongue: *the tongue is a fire, and stands for a whole world of wickedness; so the tongue can defile the whole body... no human being has learned to tame the tongue; it is restless and depraved, full of deadly poison and evil influence.*

Sinfulness, and its many forms, is a complicated construct, the Greek New Testament uses several different words to describe various wrongdoings: *a false step, an offense, a trespass, a fault, iniquity, disobedience, wickedness, and a violation of God's stated behavior.* The structure of the word *"sin"* comes from archery, and simply means *"missing the mark."* Look back to the "I–we" dichotomy. **Sin is always against God's plan**; however, some sins are against **self,** at times sins are against others: **him, her, them, those people, somebody...anybody!** To simplify the issue there are two types of sin: one that will separate you from God and one that will break partnership with the God and others. There is still another way to view bad behavior: one is a sin of commission, another a sin of omission. One is something that is done while the other is something that is left undone. All evil is against God's plan for redeemed mankind; it is, missing God's mark and the high calling for honorable living

> *13. Rid your minds of every encumbrance, keep full control of your senses, and set your hopes on the gift that is offered you when Jesus Christ appears; 14. have childlike obedience.* **Do not continue to live a life that matches the time you did not know you were controlled by the evil yearnings: 15. but show yourselves holy in all conduct; 16. because the One who called you is holy, you must be holy in all manner of living; you must be holy because the scripture declares: God is holy!** (1 Peter 1:13-16 EDNT)

A failure to forgive another may be seen as both, commission and omission. When forgiveness is absent or wrongdoing is simply overlooked or excused, this failure is a sin of omission and God will hold individuals accountable. When there is no effort to "fix the problem" it will ester and grow worse until it begins to damage others and even the body of believers. It may not be a mortal sin which would keep one out of heaven, but a failure to forgive damages the spiritual state being and weakens the current fellowship and harmony of a faith-based association. To forgive and not remember it against the offender and seek to restore and maintain unity and harmony in the fellowship is a sacred duty. Seeking full restoration with an offender is a requirement to walk in partnership with God and in full fellowship with those in your sphere of influence. All who offend others and break the peace and fellowship of a family or faith-based group are on a crooked path where misbehavior has disastrous consequences.

That is why I say, Whatever you desire, when you pray, believe that you receive it, and you will have it. 25. <u>And when you stand up to pray, forgive anything you are holding against anyone: so that your Father in heaven may forgive you your moral wrongs.</u> 26. **But if you do not forgive, neither will your Father who is in heaven forgive your transgressions.** (*Mark 11:24.-26 EDNT*)

For if you forgive men their trespasses, your heavenly Father will also forgive you: 15 **But if you forgive not men their trespasses, neither will your Father forgive your trespasses.** (Matthew 6:14-15 EDNT)

A failure to forgive creates an uncomfortable feeling and an awareness that something is wrong or missing in your life. This is called *guilt*. Wounds or words spoken in haste by a friend can linger and be recalled much later if they are not forgiven. An unforgiving spirit creates discomfort, disorder, and disease. When one does not forgive the wrongdoing of another, the guilt hangs on and aggravates and devastates the one harboring the hurt. It will also cause the downfall of others, because there is always collateral damage when relationships are strained or broken.

Why? The offended one cannot help but share the hurt with others who may not fully understand the background and antecedent cause of the situation. Only the offended ones may recall the details of both the background and the events leading up to the problem. Understanding this, forgiveness can be given, and reconciliation pursued. To fail to act quickly may open Pandora's box creating more serious difficulties.

14. Remind them of these things, solemnly witnessing before God not to fight with words, for they are not useful but bring destruction to the ones hearing. 15. Be eager to present yourself approved to God, a workman unashamed, cutting straight the word of truth. 16. But avoid blasphemous and worthless chatter: for they will cause more disobeying of the word. 17. And their teaching will eat as does gangrene: (2 Timothy 2:14-17 EDNT)

The illustration below by William G. Justice, DMin, DPhil, was found after his death in his vast collection of books on guilt and forgiveness. It clearly shows his perspective on how the burden of guilt is complex and pushes down toward destruction and how climbing the hill of difficulty toward the light of forgiveness and reconciliation can change the person willing to utilize their capacity to forgive.

—William G. Justice

What is forgiveness? A conscious decision to release feelings of resentment or vengeance toward a person or group who have harmed or offended you, regardless of whether they deserve your forgiveness. The word *"offend"* in scripture means "*caused to stumble or seduce to sin.*" Transgression may well cause the offended and others to stumble into wrongdoing. In each such situation the objective is to be a survivor who initiated reconciliation with a friend or neighbor (or even an enemy). The best way forward is to forgive, climb that hill of difficulty toward the light, forgive and be reconciled with the offender and try to remove the incident from your memory bank. One should always consider the old saying: **"To err is human; to forgive is divine!"** Always exercise the God given capacity to forgive quickly and humbly.

Jesus never defined "forgiveness" leaving the meaning to individuals. Contemporary conceptions of forgiveness have emotional dimensions. The Greek word *forgive* in New Testament, *aphiemi,* had a wide range of meanings used 146 times but translated as *forgive* only 38 times. Meanings expressed included: *to settle a debt, to leave something or someone alone, to allow action, to leave, to send away, to forgive, to desert or abandon.* Forgiveness is an action rather than a feeling; however, reconciliation is an emotional event and causes all parties to have good feelings. Jesus and others taught that forgiveness was to be offered openly and straightforwardly. Receiving forgiveness is the burden of the offended not the offender.

Why? The forgiver is acting with godly strength and must convince the trespasser that reconciliation is a benefit to both parties. Rejection of forgiveness is not equivalent to *"dusting off your shoes"* and walking away from those who reject the Gospel. In the case of faith-based people, forgiving is dealing with a believer and the responsibility is greater. Should the offended reject forgiveness and refuse to participate in reconciliation, they are then to be treated as an unbeliever. This is a bad place to be and is totally unnecessary.

> *16. **Acknowledge your failures and side steps one to another, and pray for yourselves and for one another, that you may be made spiritually whole again**. When a righteous person prays fervently there is great power in prayer. 19. My band of believers, if any of you do stray from the true path, and one turn you about. 20. **let the brother know, that he who turns one back from the error of his way into the right path, covers many faults and makes him safe, restoring his usefulness to the congregation**. (James 5:16-7;19-20 EDNT)*

> *14. Pursue harmony with all men, and strive for that consecration without which no man shall see the Lord: 15. watch that no one misses the grace of God; lest any cause for animosity grow up to trouble you, and thereby many be corrupted; 16. watch that no one falls into sexual impurity or follows a blasphemous person, as Esau, who for a scrap of food gave up the rights of the first born. 17. Afterward, he was eager enough to have the blood related honor, but was rejected: he had no opportunity to change his mind, although he sought that blessing with tears. **Have the preserving principle of divine grace in your hearts, and live in peace with one another**. (Hebrews 12:14-17 EDNT)*

> <u>**6. Herein you are triumphant, even if it is presently necessary to be saddened by trials of many sorts, 7. this must be so you can give proof of your faith,**</u>

a more precious thing than gold tested by fire, this proof will bring you praise, and glory, and honor when Jesus Christ is revealed. *8. You never saw Him, but you learned to love Him, although you do not see Him, you believed in Him. And rejoice with triumphant joy. 9. You are receiving that which faith ultimately brings, the salvation of the Soul.* (1 Peter 1:8-9 EDNT)

Communion is only for believers
walking in fellowship with God and
commemorating the death
and resurrection of Jesus;
it includes what the Greeks called
"koinonia" and transliterated as
communion, community, joint
participation, stewardship, sharing,
and spiritual intimacy.

7

EXAMINATION and SOLIDARITY at Communion

A Mountain Man living alone in a cabin, became tired of his own cooking, and decided he needed assistance with his life. He went to the Trading Post and discussed his options: send for a mail order bride or buy a cookbook with recipes. His living environment was not ready to accommodate a wife and ordering a cookbook would be quicker and a less costly choice to improve his disposition and outlook on life. When the cookbook came each recipe begin with, **Take a clean dish.** There were no clean dishes in the cabin, so he returned the cookbook and ordered a mail order bride. Yes, he got busy cleaning up his living space to receive a personal partner and hopefully a better cook.

Without daily attention, life and living accumulates clutter that needs cleaning or removal to establish or improve relationships with others. Often a negative atmosphere surrounds daily life and breeds doubt, prejudice, and a false analysis of the action of others. Personal attention must be given to personal lifestyle before reaching out to others. Forgiving self for understood faults and difficult interaction with others is the place to start. There is also the need for washing the mind with the Word and improving the heart with earnest prayer. Personal initiative must be taken to prepare for a better life. Self-examination and developing a team spirit are clear prerequisite to transparent and peaceful relationships.

The process of living brings people into contact with others. Believers must be certain that this contact measures up to spiritual standards of the Word of God. Living in harmony with others, assisting them, being a moral example, and cooperating with them for the common good is the spiritual minimum. A joint believer encounter, as radii of a circle, forms the spokes of "togetherness" with God as the center. Here individuals can dwell in love, raise children, worship God, and participate in spiritual activity. This happens when people are willing to commit themselves to spiritual values and take their stand together for moral and ethical conduct.

The triangular relationship among individuals is insisted upon in the sacred writings. The person who loves God must love others, even an enemy. The closer one gets to God the more intimate and more harmonious their relationship becomes with other people. The converse is true: when one drifts away from God there is considerable deterioration in human relationships (See Figure 1, 2, and 3).

The language of prayer Jesus taught His disciples gives evidence of a collective concern for the group. Jesus taught them to pray "**Our** Father…Give **us**…forgive **us**…as **we** forgive…lead **us**…deliver **us**…." These plural pronouns are obvious. When an individual is in full fellowship with God, they have a burning desire to live peaceably with others. The problem of the unredeemed is that no amount of *"human engineering"* can simulate the spiritual dynamic of true friendship and fellowship among believers.

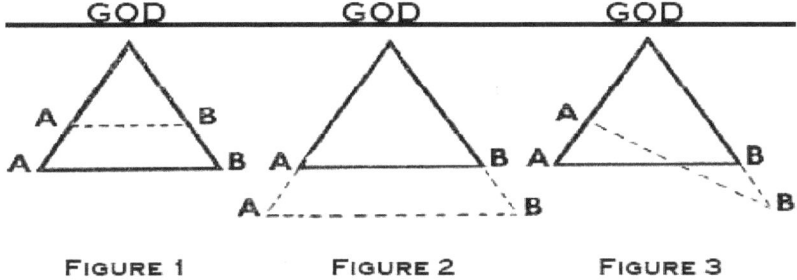

FIGURE 1 **FIGURE 2** **FIGURE 3**

TRIANGLE RELATIONSHIP. The relationship between A and B illustrated here is in direct relation to their relationship with God. Figure 1 shows that as A and B get closer to God they are closer to one another. Figure 2 illustrates the strain in human relations when both A and B drift away from God. Figure 3 shows the change that takes place when A draws closer to God and B drifts away. This situation often complicates both the spiritual life and the human relations of A and B.

There can be no spiritual fellowship until individuals have first shared a common relationship with Jesus. It must be a triangular encounter—a three-way relationship. Human beings may associate with one another in daily living, but they will never really know and understand one another until they meet together in the presence of God. God's love leaves no room for the usual bitterness that plagues and weakens human relations. A life of love causes one to see the connection between God and Man and demonstrates the real meaning of a relationship with Jesus. It is evident that the more one knows of Jesus and His love, the more love the individual will have both for both God and others.

Fellowship with God is the key to proper human relations. This is the subject of the First Epistle of John. John declared that the basis of spiritual fellowship was fellowship with the Father through a union with Jesus. Believers who live and walk in the true Light of God will have fellowship with God, and once this fellowship is established one can be assured of a satisfying relationship with others. Without fellowship with God, human relations cannot be essentially right.

Harmony in human relations often depends on what one is making of their personal life. The structure of life must be built upon the Word; however, inter-personal relations depend on (1) the climate of one's personality, (2) the standards by which others are measured, and (3) the basic motives that determine one's acts. The God-related experience meets the needs in each of these areas. When people join together in an effort to build their lives after God's plan, they are bound to get along with each other.

A wrong relationship with God is the root of all unchristian conduct. God desires that men live together in the "realm of redemption." Sin in the life of an individual causes relationship with God to be changed, and the relationship with others disturbed. Likewise, any disturbance in the personal relations of two believers hinders their spiritual fellowship with God (First Peter 3:7). It is a three-way interaction, a triangular relationship or nothing.

People often think that they are having trouble with their fellowman, when actually they themselves are out of touch with God and are in trouble spiritually. These differences often lead to the "futile fuss of talk." It should be remembered that a sinner is the victim of human nature and quarrels because of that nature. It takes the work of divine authority to correct this, but it can be done through simple faith in God. God can change the diverse fractions of human behavior into the common denominator of His grace through Jesus Christ. Transformed by the power of His Cross, the will of God becomes clearly seen, human barriers melt away, and men with varying personalities can bow together in worship and in love. It is in Jesus Christ that people get together; He is the one access route for all men to the Father.

When individuals sincerely pray about differences, they will discover that the positive virtues flowing out of their Christian love causes a joining of forces to do God's will. Find the center of the circle of relationship. There are three competing elements striving for control of the relationship triangle. These are (1) **Self** as a controlling factor deals with personality, character, and individual identity as central to the relationship, (2) **Sexual expression** used as a coping mechanism must be secondary to the primary control and must not become a gender issue but always relates to both partners and whether or not the maintenance of the relationship would collapse without sex, and (3) **Spirituality** as the crucial deciding factor in a faith-based expression as the core of the devotion and affection between the couple. Just as the Creation Trinity are three in one; so self, sex, and spirituality combine to create one relationship that is either good or bad. It depends on the relationship controller that encircles the couple.

A relationship must be built on mutual respect and a grand pursuit of happiness. The excitement is in the pursuit, the chase, the ultimate objective is never reached, but the effort continues and that is the joy of living together in a sound relationship. The founders who composed the American Constitution wrote about the "pursuit of happiness" that was a guaranteed right of all. Claim your part of this provision and walk with your mate in pursuit of the goals that will bring mutual happiness.

Find the Center

The center controls the whole circle of relationship and is the main part of and the middle point that forms the circle around a marriage. To find the center, one uses three points: it will most likely be self, sex, or a spiritual emphasis. One will be the primary point or the controlling force in the relationship, the other two will factor into finding that center or point of reference. Otherwise there will be a wobbly satellite destined to fall and be consumed by the hostile atmosphere.

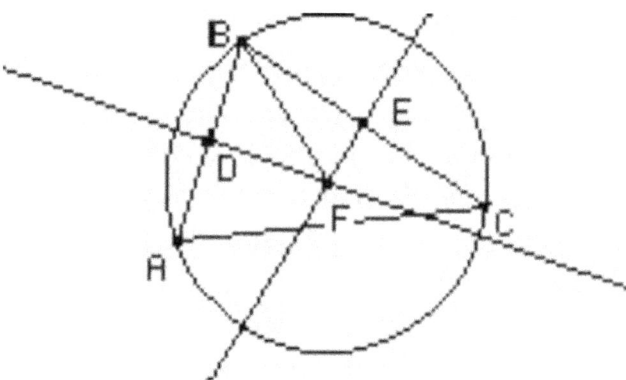

Enclose a circle about a central point of a relationship

Knowing and understanding the role of the center is essential to an adequate relationship. Whichever point is the center (self, sex, spiritual) it will control the other factors and keep them either in balance or out of balance. An out of balance relationship will deteriorate and ultimately fail.

Elements Competing for Control

The three competing elements striving for control of the relationship triangle are **(1) Self** as a controlling factor deals with personality, character, and individual identity as central to the relationship. If self were the controlling factor, the relationship would become unstable, unpredictable, and even erratic. **(2) Sexual** expression used as a coping mechanism must be secondary to the primary control and must not become a gender issue but always relates to both partners and whether or not the maintenance of the relationship would collapse without sex. If sex becomes the primary control, the relationship will be short-lived. **(3) Spirituality** as the crucial deciding factor in a faith-based expression as the core of the devotion and affection between the couple. Provided the locus of control is a spiritual emphasis or agreed upon faith-based principles and goals, and others are left out of the circle, the relationship should become stable and maintain a permanent orbit above the cares of life that so easily overwhelm a weak marriage relationship.

Application to a Relationship

The technical procedure has a practical connection to relationship building. With (B) being the apex power/influence and (A) being spouse A and (C) being spouse C find the midpoint on line AB and CB which is relational connection to the apex and label the midpoints of AB (Destiny that relates to Providence) and CB (Eternity that relates to perpetuity). Then construct a line perpendicular to line AB at point Destiny and a line perpendicular to line CB at point Eternity. Label this point of intersection of the two perpendicular bisectors point (F) (Future). This is the midpoint of the circle that is constructed from the midpoint of the couple's relationship to the apex which will determine the Future of the relationship. Now the center has been determined. Next construct line (FB) to connect the Future to the apex and this becomes the radius that determines the range of effectiveness or influence that holds the relationship together. Notice that this establishes a relationship between (Destiny) providence and (Eternity) perpetuity.

Relationship is a limited circle that contains only the couple and the influential power source and excludes all others who are not signers of the contract or partakers of the covenant agreement. This is where the leaving and cleaving enter a marriage relationship. Now this relationship is on solid footing with providence and perpetuity connected and unless some outside force intervenes to disturb the "perfect union" things will go as well as humanly possible until death suspends the earthly part of the journey.

Just as the Creation Trinity are three in one; so self, sex, and spirituality combine to create one relationship that is either good or bad. It depends on the relationship controller that encircles the couple. This means the couple must agree on which of these three forces will be in the driver's seat and which ones will be the backseat drivers offering suggestions from time to time. This depends on which one of the three is strong enough to control the relationship and be used to enclose and limit the size of the relationship circle. Remember there will be enough conflict among these three without adding others to the mix. Keep the issues inside the circle.

When individuals are transformed by God's redemptive love and are gathered into a spiritual community, they are eager to cooperate for edification and evangelism. As the Spirit weaves the scarlet thread of redemptive benefits into the pattern of interpersonal relations, believers grow in spiritual companionship and in concern for one another.

A dynamic, growing, transforming spiritual experience compels individuals into wholesome companionship with other believers. Redeemed individuals work together in group life and activity, but always remain an individual on a personal basis with God. Walking with other believers in Christian fellowship is a searching experience. The believer accepts this new companionship as new creatures in Christ, and forgiven sins are forgotten. While there remains a clear distinction between persons, yet believers set apart from the world assume a common identity and bond of peace in the Spirit. Fellowship that is spiritual sanctifies all of life and creates a oneness among believers. This God created unity is not meant to make believers into unhappy satellite souls burdened by the monotony of similarity, but it is concerned with the believers' common devotion to Jesus, mutual fellowship, and beneficial united spiritual action.

The spiritual life of believers could not long remain a solitary thing. They must not only have a relationship with God, but they must have fellowship with other believers. The spiritual experience becomes void if it is deprived of fellowship with other believers. Should believers discover one another in an unchurched community, they should not think of the church as being *"back home,"* but they should unite to function as a vital part of the living church. Saints experience great joy when they unite and then watch the emerging congregation grow, especially when this growth is out of their having gathered together for worship.

Believers dwelling together in fellowship, form a spiritual community that demonstrates the love of Jesus or others. Since love must first be learned by experiencing love, God teaches us to love by first loving Him. *"He that loveth is born of God and knows God."* The believer finds a basic need for inter-personal love and companionship met by the divine love and spiritual fellowship. Because of God's indwelling love, believers love one another with fervency and a purity unattainable by any other faith-based system on earth.

There is a creativeness in spiritual companionship. God ministers His own strength to a believer by sending assistance through a fellow believers. The primary concern of God's plan for perfecting the saints is to make the individual in the image of Christ. When believers assist one another in spiritual growth, they share with God the effort to make individuals in His image and likeness.

Faith-based individuals have a right to expect consensus in their joint activity. Sincere mature believers will be agreeable and respectable to one another even when they disagree. In other words, they can disagree agreeably. They should move through a problem-solving experience with assurance that God is guiding their action. When the solution is found, they should say *"This seemed good to the Spirit and to us."* This is spiritual consensus. Observing how believers meet the problems of life should be an evangelizing, convicting experience for those who do not follow Jesus.

Christian communion was a central part of God's Plan to bring men and God together and to bring about the reconciliation between humanity brought on by the curse of sin. The inspired Word is always the criterion by which the thoughts and behavior of men are evaluated. In addition to the regenerating and sanctifying power of truth, human beings need the enlightenment that comes as the Holy Spirit illuminates the preserved Word and reveals its relative meaning to a life application. The human heart is the Lord's writing table to inscribe the holy truths by which believers must live and work. These hidden truths are revealed in moral and ethical behavior involving both friends and foes.

Communion is a time of reaching deeply into these truths for both assurance and guidance. The hidden truth in the heart enables believers to grasp the meaning of personal guilt related to individual errors of omission and conduct that my have affected others negatively. These truths also cause an awareness of the necessity to forgive others their offenses directly and without narrow-mindedness. The truths written on the heart provide strength and guidance to keep on the straight and narrow way that leads to life eternal.

It is clear from scripture that God provides direction once, but guidance often. God has a purpose for each life, and each event in that life, but the human element always frustrates the divine plan and there is a failure to understand what God is doing in each situation. When a believer does not know what or why God is permitting a certain situation, this is a signal that the closeness to Jesus has diminished. In (John 15:15) Jesus *"a servant does not know what his master is doing."* With this declaration, *Jesus changed their designation from "servant" to "friend" and shared "No longer do I call you servants, because a servant does not know what his master is doing, but I will call you friends."* It seems there is a place of friendship with Jesus where one may fully understand what God is doing in their lives. The words to an old hymn, **Draw Me Nearer** (1875) by Frances J. Crosby provides direction and action toward a consecration to reach that friendship level with Jesus.

> *I am Thine, O Lord, I have heard Thy voice,*
> *And it told Thy love to me;*
> *But I long to rise in the arms of faith*
> *And be closer drawn to Thee.*
>
> *Consecrate me now to Thy service, Lord,*
> *By the power of grace divine;*
> *Let my soul look up with a steadfast hope,*
> *And my will be lost in Thine.*
>
> *Oh, the pure delight of a single hour*
> *That before Thy throne I spend,*
> *When I kneel in prayer, and with Thee, my God*
> ***I commune as friend with friend*!**

Consequently, it is necessary for the believer to constantly receive spiritual guidance from the Word and the prompting of the Holy Spirit. The Word reveals the simple process: *if the believer lives in God's Light, the blood of Jesus, His Son, continues to cleanse from each sin and there is spiritual communion with God and believers.* (1 John 1:3 and 7)

Spiritual guidance comes through personal and collective prayers, confession of short comings, the singing of hymns, offering praises to God for his worth, forgiving self and others, participating in worship and communion, enjoying the fellowship of believers growing together in worship and mission. This is a history of the first three decades of the pristine church. An objective of spiritual togetherness expressed in worship and outreach is what the Greeks called *homothumadon* used only 12 times in the New Testament, ten (10) of which are in Acts; meaning *with one mind, unanimously, with one accord, emotion of the mind, with one purpose, with unanimous consent, and the principle of life.*

Worship and partaking of Holy Communion is not only a personal matter; it involves others. It must be preceded by an analysis of one's personal life and the quality of fellowship with others. All relationship difficulties must be corrected prior to communion. If wrongdoings have caused a strain on individuals, this must be fixed through forgiveness and reconciliation. Preparation for communion is part of the process of remaining current with God and others.

Participation in worship and Communion in an unworthy manner with no self-examination and confession is contrary to the sacred text. Confession of any sense of guilt and forgiveness and sincere attempts at restoration must proceed communion or one becomes spiritually powerless and physically sick. In fact, the quality of fellowship for the whole congregation can be weakened by serious relationship problems among the membership. Unconfessed sins are unforgiven, and one must embrace communion with prayer and a clean heart that has been cleansed by confession and the Word.

And in conclusion, whoever shall eat this bread and drink this cup of the Lord, in an unworthy manner, shall be guilty of violating the body and blood of the Lord. 28. **Each time let a man examine himself before he eats of that bread and drinks of that cup. 29. The reason for self-examination before eating and drinking is to prevent partaking in an unworthy manner when one does not properly consider the Lord's assembly. 30.** *For this reason many are powerless and sick among you and many die.* (1 Corinthians 11:27-30)

Often when conflict exists in a relationship, there is a failure to communicate; that is, to pass clear data from one person to another using the same encoding and decoding. When these are different there will be no understanding; consequently, the static must be removed or at lease minimized. In addition to the problems build into communication, there are innate difficulties in all relationship which require a spiritual dynamic to hold things together.

Human relationships are similar to an assorted box of chocolates, there is always the anticipation of sweetness and pleasure, but often the choice is not what was expected. At the human level this is reality; however, when one considers friendship and fellowship between believers there is an extra dose of expectation that everyone will be OK, and all will behave and comport themselves in a moral and ethical manner.

Yet, believers remain human beings and retain most of the human equation which does not always balance. Scripture asks, *"Can two walk together, except they agree on the direction?"* (Amos 3:3) And the wise man Solomon declared, *"Two are better than one, because they have a good reward for their labor. For if they fall, the one will lift up his fellow: but woe to him that is alone when he falls; for he has not another to help him up (Ecclesiastes 4:9,10)*

Worship may include confession, collect, communion and celebration. *Confession* is an individual act of admission of human weakness, the acceptance of guilt, and the affirmation of forgiveness. *Collect* is the gathering "together" of believers assembled in unity responding to personal pardon and the promises of God; a collect is both personal and collective action in prayer, praise and worship. *Communion* is only for believers walking in fellowship with God and others commemorating the death and resurrection of Jesus; it includes what the Greeks called *"koinonia" which* transliterated as *communion, community, joint participation, stewardship, sharing, and spiritual intimacy.* The first New Testament use of *koinonia* was in Peter's sermon at Pentecost (Acts 2:41-47) where the essence of *koinonia* was *a togetherness in love, faith, and encouragement.* Also, Paul used the concept to express agreement with one another, being united in purpose, and serving alongside each other based on fellowship with God and each other. (Philippians 2:1-11). Communion clearly expresses shared beliefs and common spiritual and relational expectations. It also suggests a nearness to God and a closeness to friends and remembers the death, burial and resurrection of Jesus until He returns in power and glory.

Early neglect of new converts and the teaching of children creates a weakness in theological content that causes problems with a lifestyle of discipleship and a failure to mature as a believer. The challenge of Jesus to His Followers was to *"make disciples"* as they went about their daily business and to identify each convert with the Trinity: the Father as the forgiver; the Son as the Savior; the Holy Spirit as the enabler, the guide to truth, and a *"present help in time of trouble."* When converts are not adequately initiated into the Ministry of the Godhead, their spiritual growth will be restricted, and their lifestyle may have less identification with Jesus and a limited ability to observe all that Jesus taught. Neglect in teaching converts may also cause a lack of awareness of the continuing presence of Jesus in the life of each believer, *"behold, I am with you always, even unto the end of the world."* This was a clear promise to new disciples who were adequately identified through baptism with the Trinity, taught to observe all that Jesus did and taught, and understood that His Presence was with them and would always be present until the end of the world. Armed with the complete teaching of Jesus and an identification with the Trinity, they could practice the presence of Jesus and always know He was "a present help in times of trouble."

When water baptism becomes a one-time formal ceremony for others to observe without the complete teaching/learning to be identified with the role of the Trinity in their life, the Candidate has been shortchanged and will demonstrate a weak understanding and value of Holy Communion and other functions designed to keep a believer current in relationship with God; such as, freely giving, worship participation, using their time, talent, and resources for advancing the kingdom, ongoing fellowship, and outreach efforts for the cure of souls. Since Water Baptism and Holy Communion are two significant sacraments instituted by Jesus, Candidates are not prepared to take on a mature missional lifestyle and true worship with full involvement of the Trinity in their life and worship.

Communion as a concept includes the sharing or exchanging of intimate thoughts and feelings at a spiritual level. Communion as a sacrament or formal ceremonial procedure during a worship experience is structured to memorials the suffering, death, and resurrection of Jesus. It is an intimate process designed to demonstrate a spiritual union between Jesus and believers.

There are two basic positions relative to the bread and wine: some believe in *transubstantiation* where the elements are transformed by the Spirit into the actual body and blood of Jesus; others who reject actual transubstantiation, believe in the *transforming* power of communion when the bread and wine are received with a clean heart and the elements are properly discerned; that is, distinguished (1) *bread* representing the broken Body of Jesus sacrificed for physical healing and the *wine* represents the New Testament sealed in the blood of Jesus for the spiritual needs of salvation and continued forgiveness.

A Service of Communion has three objectives: (1) a call or invite to those who have received salvation to celebrate the death, resurrection and return of Jesus. (2) to provide opportunity for those with a clean heart who properly discern the Lord's body to receive the healing power of wounds and strips of Jesus. (3) to encourage participants to present themselves for service until Jesus returns in glory and power at the end of the age. There were dire consequences to those who received the elements unworthily or carelessly by not distinguishing the purpose and value of each element: the bread and the wine as they relate to the Lord's Body, the church, in maintaining health and a current state of forgiveness and readiness for spiritual growth. (See 1 Corinthians 11:1-34)

8

TOGETHERNESS and FAITHFULNESS in Worship

When the unworthiness of man is measured against the worth and value of the all-powerful God, the pathway to salvation becomes unobstructed and a willingness to accept the mercy and grace of a loving God becomes active. Redemption of the soul occurs with a confession of sin is combined with simple faith in divine promises. Following the gift of eternal life, the believer grows in grace and reverence toward God and becomes active in heartfelt worship.

In accepting the gift of eternal life, one must respect the supernatural power of God as an object of esteem and devotion. To honor the source of salvation is to respect the sacrifice of Jesus that was necessary to bring the message of saving grace to mankind. As one grows in faith and knowledge, the grasp of the significance of redemption and gift of eternal life becomes more obvious and the desire to honor the worth and value of God develops. The individual becomes aware that an innate capacity to humbly submit to the worship of God exists within their mortal being. A natural and logical response to the value of God's gift is to seek opportunity to honor and respect the significance of God in all aspects of life.

A newly convert realizes that their life has purpose and that God is at the vortex of the drastic change that has modified their outlook on life and others. The attitude toward self and others has changed, the desire to associate with like-minded individuals becomes clear and the excitement of existence becomes an overpowering dominance of a moral and spiritual life.

New association with others provides the force of group dynamics to enhance their witness of drastic changes in attitude and lifestyle. The process of maturation is accelerated, and positive contributions are forthcoming to family, friends, and regular spiritual fellowship as one lives a life of obedience to the will of God.

Man can do nothing to put himself in right relationship with God. Rather, the grace of God must be the starting point. A spiritual life is lived from a clean heart upward to God and outward to others. There is an earnestness toward God that seeks guidance and assistance. When these are present in the heart, the duties to God and the obligations to others become normal duties. They become the rule of life which the believer embraces with devotion and delightful determination.

Obeying and serving God naturally leads one to the sincere worship of God. Worship has to do with the worth of God in one's life. Believers will see "value added" in every area of life and pursue spiritual guidance. Walking sincerely before God in an attitude of devotion is essential to doing God's will and enjoying spiritual health. God is adored and exalted by a consistent life of reverence, pure thoughts, prayer, regular Bible study, sincere meditation, public worship, and unselfish daily living and service to others. Worship at any time and any place is simply responding to the upward pull of devotion to God and prompt acceptance of divine guidance.

The early disciples of Jesus were taught to pray: *"Thy will be done."* (Matthew 6:10) Trusting God is inherently delightful. One who respects the Creator God should be able to defend their faith with confidence, bear spiritual discipline without murmuring, and rejoice in the hope of eternal fellowship with God.

There must be a balance among these areas of self development: (1) In the *physical* must be a balanced between work and rest; neither must suffer at the expense of the other. (2) The *mental* development should have a balance between study, or gathering information, and the use of facts in answering questions or solving problems that relate to life and service. (3) In the realm of the *spiritual*, there ought to be a balance between profession and practice. Spiritual development should bring about balance between the contrasting elements of firmness and kindness, faith and works, worship and service, hearing and doing. The spiritual must first be activated by New Testament principles and consideration of self and others from which the practical and proper action should be spontaneous. (4) In the area of *social* development, the balance must be between perfecting of personality and the cultivation of friendship with others. This self-development and social improvement must then be used to the better good and spiritual advantage of all concerned.

A believer should not only be attached to Christ, they ought to also have fellowship with other believers. The abiding influence of the gathered saints is essential to maintain a present tense relationship with God. Scripture clearly teaches that the spiritual experience is strengthened by believer fellowship and weakened by the lack of solidarity. An alliance with other believers in the worship and work of the kingdom enables continued fellowship with Christ.

Fellowship with a faith-based group involves sincere connectedness with others of like mindedness and lifestyle with thankfulness and persistence. Inclusion responsibilities include being faithful to God, living a clean moral life, remaining loyal and steadfast in faith, sharing in service to others, assembling together and encouraging one another. (Colossians 3:15, 16)

In Creation, God gave man a mind with which to think, a heart with which to love, a will with which to choose, and a soul which would be desirous of worship and fellowship. Mankind, all God's creation, alone possesses the capacity and desire to worship God. Worship is that necessary nourishment and pleasure that a spiritual person needs to grow in grace and benevolence. Worship is acknowledging the worth and value of a spiritual connectedness with God and the opportunity to participate in the service of others.

People can worship God anywhere at any time, but generally, they worship best in groups. Group activity becomes less satisfying as the group becomes larger. This should be a warning to the super-church. To survive, large congregations must have many small active groups: strong family emphasis, effective classes, prayer groups, study groups, youth groups, fellowship groups, outreach groups, and other such groups and activities as needed in the community. Individuals who fail to participate in public worship usually will not have the desire or the courage to maintain family devotions or personal meditation and prayer in the home. The believer has an obligation to God, self, family, friends, the lost, and to be consistent in private and public worship. Active participation in the life of the faith-based is necessary to keep the connection current and meaningful. Without regular participation, interest will decline and the spiritual unity of the believer with others will deteriorate.

When the frequency of participation decreases, a decline in the strength of the fellowship will follow. As a result, individuals become "neutral" in their feelings toward one another. Even when the early believers were together almost daily, the writer of Hebrews warned against *"forsaking the assembling of ourselves together."* An additional injunction followed; *"And so much the more as you see the day approaching."* Gathering together with other like-minded believers will keep the worship of God and the active connectedness with others vital to fellowship for outreach and positive social change.

Heartfelt connectedness must be the motivating force for participation in faith-based activities. A spiritual test of worship causes the believer to ask: "Does my participation make me more Christ-like in attitude and behavior?" Am I merely being a spectator at a worship service without receiving a personal benefit? Participation must be for the true worship of God and should never become a substitute for personal devotion. Participating ought to re-enforce the believer 's spiritual behavior.

This is suggested when Jesus spoke of a man who brought his gift to the altar and remembered that he and his brother were in disagreement. Jesus declared that this worshiper must first reconcile with the other person and then his worship would have meaning, and God would receive his worship and gifts at the altar. (Matthew 5:23,24)

> *11. Now may God Himself and our Father, and the Lord Jesus Christ, direct our journey to you. 12. And may the Lord increase you and cause you to abound in love one toward another, and toward all men, even as we do toward you: 13. in order that He may strengthen your hearts so you may be blameless in holiness before God, who is our Father, at the coming of our Lord Jesus with all His saints.* (1 Thessalonians 3:11-13 EDNT)

Congregational attitude and action in worship are driven by the sacredness of forgiveness and the blessedness of reconciliation. Attitude is the predisposition to behave in a particular way in response to the predisposition. It is sacred because God, the Heavenly Father, sent His Son to be crucified for the salvation of mankind: that all might be forgiven and worship the One and True God as believers. Blessed because His forgiveness empowers the believer's capacity to behave toward others with a forgiving spirit; thus, the capacity to forgive prompts a willingness to forgive the weakness and shortcomings of others and seeks to act in a manner that enhances their ability to grow in grace and behave with maturity.

Worship then is the capacity to acknowledge the saving grace and extended mercy provided by the sacred redemption through the sacrifice of Jesus. True worship provides the individual with a spiritual mindset which will minimize the human misery and maximize the end of the journey. Worship reminds one that the end is worth the journey. Paul who suffered greatly for his outreach to the Gentiles was clear on this issue: *I consider the sufferings we now endure not worthy to be compared with the glory about to be revealed in us.* (Romans 8:18)

There is a sacredness in forgiveness when expressed by the offended; it is God-like to forgive others. Especially without the mortal sacrifice, yet there are crosses to bear and burdens to carry. Carrying the load of wrongdoings perpetuated by another is a heavy burden. Without forgiving others their misdeeds, the load simply gets heavier. Without forgiveness the burden grows. Maturity demands forgiveness:

> *1. Brethren, if a man should make an unintended error due to weakness, you who are regenerated, repair and adjust him with a teachable spirit; continue considering yourself, lest you also be tempted to make a false step.2. Practice in sharing the heavy burdens of others, and you will fulfill the principle of Christ. (Galatians 6:1-2 EDNT)*

> *8. Finally, you must think the same thoughts, share difficulties with one another, having automatic interdependence with brotherly kindness; be tender-hearted and humble-minded: 9. you must not repay injury with injury, or hard words with hard words, but bless those who curse you. For you were called to give kind words to others and come to a well-spoken eulogy at the end. 10. For the one wishing to love life and see prosperous days, let him avoid an evil tongue and cunning words. 11. Habitually avoid evil and do good things; let him seek and follow peace. 12. Because the eyes of the Lord watch over the righteous, and his ears listen to their prayers: but the Lord looks directly into the eyes of wrongdoers. (1 Peter 3:8-12 EDNT)*

> Believers are to be shining lights on the road less traveled and enlighten fellow travelers along the journey.

9

TRANSPARENCY and RESTORATION with Believers

Forgiveness is a theoretical challenge: is it an *emotion* or a *behavior*? Perhaps it is both *internal* and *external,* both an individual and collective matter. Aristotle, an Ancient Greek philosopher, who is considered one of the great thinkers in ethics used the term "*sungnome*" together with mercy in dealing with a wrongdoer. *Sungnome* meant *sympathy, pity, fellow-feeling, pardon,* and *excuse.* Most scholars understand Aristotle's use of *sungnome* to be close to the current meaning of *forgiveness*, mercy or clemency. The concept was an immanent critique discussion of culture to deal with contradictions as opposed to a transcendental approach.

The scriptural construct assumes that evil as a malicious and hateful force overtakes an offender and the divine means for disengaging this forceful influence is forgiveness by the offended and God. There will be no reconciliation without clear and specific forgiveness. Paul instructs young Timothy to avoid all arguments "...*the servant of the Lord must not struggle with arguments; but behave kindly toward all men, teaching appropriately with unwearied tolerance, 25. understanding those who offend in order to instruct properly; if perhaps God will change their mind to acknowledge the truth; 26. having been captured by the will of God they may remove themselves from the trap of the devil.* (2 Timothy 2:24-26 EDNT)

To forgive is an *act* primarily for the forgiver to have peace of mind and let go any vindictiveness against the offender. Secondarily, forgiving is a *process* to bring people together for reconciliation to end suffering and produce dignity and harmony in both personal and group relationships. God's forgiveness comes during this process.

> *1.Brethren, if a man should make an unintended error due to weakness, you who are regenerated, repair and adjust him with a teachable spirit; continue considering yourself, lest you also be tempted to make a false step. 2. Practice in sharing the heavy burdens of others, and you will fulfill the principle of Christ.* (Galatians 6:1-2 EDNT)

> *18. All things are of God, who has brought us together in Himself by Jesus Christ, and has given to us the ministry of bringing people together; 19. how that God was in Christ bringing together the world to Himself, not counting their false steps and blunders against them; and has committed us to speak intelligent words that bring man and God together. 20. Now seeing we are representatives for Christ, as though God did make His appeal through us: we implore you in Christ's stead, come together with God.* (2 Corinthians 5:18-20 EDNT)

It would be good to remember an old Proverb, *"Go often to the house of your friends, because weeds soon choke an unused path."* All relationships require openness and occasional over-hauling to refurbish and maintain a positive connection. Currency of any connection with associates requires constant adjustment of both attitude and action. The human element always gets in the way of honest linkage and association with others. Few are mature enough to maintain a seamless bond with close friends. There is always need for minor tweaking and fine-tuning of any enduring relationship. Scripture is clear-cut, *"Do not let the sun go down on your aggravation or permit little things to provoke angry words or action."* It is not what happens in a relationship that matters; it is the way one handles what happens that makes the difference. There must be agreement on direction and action for individuals to travel a path to transparent relationship.

Believers are to be shining lights on the road less traveled and enlighten fellow travelers along the journey. Transparency is the issue: the reflected light of forgiveness must not come from moral darkness. Attitude, facial expressions, and tone of voice must unambiguously show an honest and sincere spirit. This is the only way forgiveness will move to restoration.

> *7. For one who has oversight as the steward of God must be beyond reproach, not stubbornly self-willed, not easily angered, not given to wine, or one who comes to blows, nor greedy after material gain. 8. But hospitable, a lover of good things, sensible, just, holy, self-controlled, 9. holding to the faithful word according to the teaching, that he may be able by healthy teaching both to exhort and to convince the contradicting ones.* (Titus 1:7-9 EDNT)

Perhaps each believer should assume responsibility for mending broken fences or building a bridge over troubled waters. Instead of freeze-framing a relationship by permitting shadows to linger and prevent one from seeing the clear path ahead. Believer must be the reflected light of God's love shinning on the pathway and revealing the stumbling blocks which could hinder straightforward progress. The reflected light must not come from moral darkness, but should be the bright light of truth. Fear may say, *"I cannot see what lies in the shadows, I will stay where I am. Better safe than sorry!"* But wisdom shines the true light of awareness that God is in charge provided the prayer of relinquishment is invoked and both parties permit God's light to show the way forward.

The ministry of reconciliation works when both the offended and the offender work together and accept a spiritual solution: which is transparent forgiveness and straightforward reconciliation. Provided Freud's assumptions were correct, all excess in defending a position in an argument will hinder the final resolution of the problem. There must be both physical and emotional restraint to solve relational difficulties. Permitting the spiritual light of God's presence to shine on the problem is the best way forward.

How is your reflected light (albedo)? It literally means white and technically it is the rate of reflected light from a surface based on the total light falling upon that surface. For example, the earth's moon has no light of its own. What is seen is the reflected light, the albedo, of the sunlight as it is thrown back or returned toward the sun. That is what is seen from the earth. The moon absorbs much of the light and only a small part is reflected back into the atmosphere. Are you reflecting light to others? How is your spiritual *albedo*? Light is the absence of darkness. Are you reflecting the Divine Light to the shadows of relationships? Can two walk together without agreeing on the direction? (Amos 3:3).

> *5. This then is the message which we have heard of Him, and announce to you, that God is light, and no darkness can find a place in Him. 6. If we say that we have fellowship with Him, and at the same time walk in darkness, we are not living the truth: 7. but if we walk in the light, as He is in the light, we have fellowship one with another, and the blood of Jesus Christ His Son cleanses us from all sin.* (1 John 1:5-7 EDNT)

Disagreement in any relationship brings moral darkness to those involved. *"Take care that the reflected light does not come from moral darkness."* Believers are to let their light shine, not only to the lost world, but to the body of believers by receiving spiritual light, absorbing some and reflecting the rest to others. You have a choice: you can be "good" or a "good bad example." No man who lights a lamp puts it in a closet, nor under a box, but on a lamp stand so all may clearly see.

> *34. The lamp of the body is the eye: therefore, when your eye is focused your whole body has light; but when your eye is morally bad, your body is full of darkness. 35. Take care that the reflected light in you does not come from moral darkness. 36. If you have light for the body with the absence of darkness, the whole shall be light, as when a candle shines brightly in the dark.* (Luke 11:33-36 EDNT)

Some years ago, a teacher of a Men's Bible Class ran for the U.S. Congress and was elected. It concerned me because we would lose his local influence. He drove from D.C. back to Beckley, WV to teach the class until he was elected to the U.S. Senate. I wrote Robert C. Byrd a letter about his leaving the Bible Class for busy government work, he responded, *"My little light shines brightly in the darkness of Washington, DC."*

Later it was my privilege to hear Senator Byrd speak at a Gideon's meeting. He gave the details about the Great Wall of China. The wall was 4,160 miles across Northern China and a structure large enough to be seen from the moon with the naked eye. Wall construction started as far back as Chinese recorded history. Prisoners of war, convicts, soldiers, civilians and family farmers provided the labor. Many Chinese stories speak of parted lovers and men dying of starvation and disease working on the construction. Materials used for the wall, were whatever could be found nearby: clay, stone, willow branches, reeds, sand, and the bodies of the dead.

Everyone listened closely as Senator Byrd told of the years it took to build the wall and the cost of material and lives. Particularly, how workers who died on the job were entombed in the wall. The wall was built to keep China's enemies from attacking sections of the country. History reveals that the all worked well when the country was strong. Only when a dynasty was weakened from within, were invaders from the north able to advance and over-power the local people, subjugate and take control of their lives. In the many years since the wall was completed, not a single invader ever breached the wall; they did not have to scale or break it down, they simply bribed the keepers of the gates.

Individual believers and their relationships are the last line of defense against Satan's onslaughts against faith-based entities seeking to advance the good news of redemption. Strong leadership and solid relationships are the last bulwark to protect the beacon of light coming from the faith-based lampstands. In reality, no wall of protection is stronger than the individuals who guard the gates. It is not whether or not faith-based relations are strong enough to protect the ongoing kingdom ministry; the real question is where are the leaders to stand in the gap and guard the gates and shine light on both the strength and weakness of the faith-based entities. When strong guards are ready, God's Light will shine and the work of God will advance. Strong believers make strong and well-supported faith-based instructions.

> *23. But be on guard: behold, I have fore-warned you about everything. 24. But in those days, after the time of trouble, the sun shall be darkened, and the moon will give not reflected light,* (Mark 1:23-24 EDNT)

> *21. When a strong man is armed and guards his homestead, his goods are safe: 22. But when a stronger one overpowers him, he takes all the weapons in which he trusted, and divides up the plunder. 23. He who is not with me is against me: and those who do not gather the sheep, scatters them.* (Luke 11:22-23 EDNT)

In relationship difficulties, there are no simple solutions or easy answers. Psychologists and counseling enterprises, together with sectarian theologians, legal negotiators have locked up the secrets and thrown away the keys. Social workers and family grievance workers have buried the combination code to personal dispute settlements deep within the pages of family law and judicial procedures that require years of specialized knowledge to unlock. Sadly, organized religion often leaves personal and property disputes to the lawyers. Scripture has a plan:

> *…if your brother shall transgress, go in private and speak about his weakness: if he listens, you have gained your brother. 16. But if he will not listen, then take one or two more with you, so that each word may be confirmed by*

two or three witnesses. 17. And if he refuses to listen to them, tell it to an assembly: but if he refuses to listen to the assembly, let him be to you as a disbeliever...
(Matthew 18:15-17 EDNT)

Notwithstanding the difficulties in personal disputes, faith-based people must not see the complication but take a fresh view of the sophistication of the process. The secrets, the keys, and the combination code to spiritual friendship and fellowship are all clearly presented in sacred scripture. Using God's Plan is free; perusing God's written material is not locked away in a bank vault or catalogued in a public library. God's Word is freely offered for consistent study and persistent practice: good results of the effort are promised to all who will read, listen, learn, and act. Provided colleagues and friends agree to walk together on the right path, good things are bound to happen.

3. Let nothing be done through argument or excessive pride; but in true humility let each value others more than themselves. 4. Look not after your own interests, but practice looking after the interest of others. 5. Let your disposition and thoughts be the same as Christ Jesus:

(Philippians 1:3-5 EDNT)

Dr. David A. Anderson, the founder and senior pastor of Bridgeway Community Church, is considered a leading authority on reconciliation based on problems of race, wealth, culture, and faith. His book, *Gracism: The Art of Inclusion,* provides a Christian alternative to secular affirmative action through the Tenets of Gracism. These precepts may be used in the process of reconciliation at all levels of forgiveness, integration and building bridges for inclusion. It was my privileged to participate in both a personal and corporate session where Dr. Anderson's principles of Gracism were repeated to each other; *to wit*:

I will lift you up,
I will share with you,
I will stand with you,
I will consider you,
I will celebrate with you,
I will cover you,
I will honor you.

Can two people walk together
without agreeing on the direction?

(Amos 3:3)

[See APPENDIX – D – WOUND WASH]

"To err is human; to forgive is divine!"

10

HARMONY and WITNESS in the Workplace

"TRUE FRIENDS PUT ENOUGH TRUST IN YOU TO TELL YOU OPENLY OF YOUR FAULTS."

— C.H. Spurgeon

Accomplishment in the workplace requires one to be mature enough to forgive the perceived wrongs of others. Groups, organizations and businesses are all made up of individuals who have their own problems and this causes difficulties in the daily workplace environment. Forgiveness shows the maturity and moral character of colleagues and becomes an authentication of the positive influence of leadership.

> *5. Let your way of life be free from the love of money; and be content with the things you have: for He said, I will never leave you, nor forsake you. 6. So we may with fluency of speech say,* **The Lord is my helper, and I will not fear what man can do to me.** *(Hebrews 13:5-6 EDNT)*

Barton Green in *Between the Lines and Spaces* (2009), recorded a good example of workplace forgiveness. Susan Ashton, a great singer, shared a difficult time in the lyrics of a song. Her maturity and moral character were authenticated by a forgiving spirit and deep admiration of someone for their qualities and accomplishments. There are many transformative benefits in respecting others; it contributes to satisfaction in their work and causes one to be more engaged and productive. Susan's attitude was well expressed in the lyrics of a song.

Her words *"Going more than halfway to forgive"* and a strong vocal expression spoke clearly of her willingness to reduce the stress and repair the relationship with a colleague.

I know we don't see eye to eye
We've let angry hearts flare
And the bitter words fly
The common ground we used to share.
Is harder to find but I believer that it's still there.

I don't know if now is the time
To surrender the silence
Between your heart and mine
But the love that I've chosen
Cries out to be spoken
Leaving the heartache behind.

We must reach out beyond justice to mercy
Going more than halfway to forgive
It doesn't matter who's to blame
The love that I have for you
Is still the same.

A tender voice is calling me
To that place of compassion
Where hearts run pure and free
Where the hunger for vengeance
Gives way to repentance
Where love will teach us to see.

— Susan Ashton

The death of Muhammad Ali was a shock to America. This present issue was not advanced until he had been honored for his achievements in life. However, watching his funeral Ceremony, Ali was recognized by the world as a man of faith. Then I remembered the words a friend shared years ago about Cassias Clay/Muhamad Ali. Lewis J. Willis, sat by Muhammad Ali on a flight out of Atlanta soon after the boxer converted to Islam and changed his name. Mr. Willis asked him why he made the switch from Christianity to Islam. His response was shocking. **"There was no challenge in Christianity; Islam gave me a way to change the world."**

Muhammad Ali was confident in his statement, firm in his conviction, and satisfied with his decision. Who failed Cassias Clay? In his hour of glory, he made a drastic switch from the teachings of his Christian Mother. Did someone fail to lead him to a personal experience with Christ? Who missed an opportunity to harness this strong voice as a fervent witness for Christianity? Where was the man of the house? Where was the mother's pastor?

True believers can change the world one person and one day at a time. The big question, **"How many**

other Mother's sons will slip through the cracks and become a spokes-person in the market place for another religion?" Christianity must compete for the minds, souls and hearts of the young in the marketplace to remain viable in the Twenty-first Century. What about missed chances? What has been done recently to advance the Cause of Christ? Do you know a young person in your community or your faith-based group who needs guidance to become a follower of Jesus? Don't miss an opportunity to witness to God's saving grace. The old adage remains true, ***"Opportunity equals obligation."***

Faith provides a means to change individuals and the world. *"Therefore, if any man be in Christ, he is a new creation: observe, the old things have passed away; all things have become new.* (2 Corinthians 5:17 EDNT)

True conversion works; it is about face and moving in an opposite direction. Anything less is not a valid transformation. The only hope for a viable mono-theistic, faith-based worship and witness is an internal redirection of the heart and soul that brings with it a missional lifestyle and personal protest against the immorality of society. Such redirection will bring both a commitment to the cardinal tenets of sacred writings and a spirit of cooperation and teamwork among believers.

Recently in Trinidad a young Hindu asked, *"Why does your religion not teach reincarnation?"* My simple answer, *"A basic tenant of Christianity is Reincarnation."* "You see, 'if anyone be in Christ, he is a new creation, old things have passed away and all things have become new.' As believers, we fix our eternal destiny before death.... there is certainty about our place in eternity."

When Paul was writing the second personal letter to the converts in Corinth, he was clear that looking at the Cross through the Empty Tomb enabled a better grasp of the new creation in and through a resurrected Jesus. The Resurrection of Jesus, which guaranteed His Deity, became the foundation for the "new creation" at conversion.

> *16. In conclusion, we should know no one after the flesh: I affirm that we have known Christ after the flesh, yet henceforth we know Him no more as a mortal man.* **(Paul explained the "new creation" and the missional lifestyle of believers:)** *17. Therefore if any man be in Christ, he is a new creation: observe, the old things have passed away; all things have become new. 18. All things are of God, who has brought us together in Himself by Jesus Christ, and has given to us the ministry of bringing people together; 19. how that God was in Christ bringing together the world to Himself, not counting their false steps and blunders against them; and has committed us to speak intelligent words that bring man and God together. (2 Corinthians 5:16-19 EDNT)*

Forgiveness and reconciliation does not come easily; they both require divine assistance to accomplish. Paul writes about this in Philippians:

> *13. For it is God working in you to make you both willing and able to do His good pleasure. 14. Do all things without grumbling and disagreements: 15. that you may be above suspicion and unblemished, the children of God, with an untarnished reputation, in the midst of a warped and twisted nation, where you shine as lights in the world; 16. holding forth the word of life; (Philippians 2:13-16 EDNT)*

The act of forgiving is the last thing an offender may expect of one they have treated badly. Individuals normally expect the same behavior from others as they express themselves: a common reversal of the Golden Rule. This is what the old English called **equivalent retaliation** or *tit-for-tat*. This continues the conflict and is based on the carnal nature of human beings: *"to err is human."* It often comes as a surprise when a forgiving spirit is expressed by a colleague who has been damaged or offended by word or deed by others. The Word is clear that retaliation is not the path to forgiveness and harmony in the workplace.

> *1. Finally, we urge you in the Lord Jesus, that, as you have received instructions from us as to how you must behave to please God, so you should follow the pattern more and more. 2. For you know the instructions we gave you through the Lord Jesus; 3. for this is the will of God,...* 6. **none of you should be excessive, and take advantage of his brother in business dealings. Because the Lord is the avenger of such excess, as our testimony forewarned you.** *7. For God did not call us on the basis of impurity but in the sphere of consecration. 8 Therefore he who rejects this instruction does not reject man, but rejects the God who gave us the Holy Spirit. (1Thessalonians 4:1-8 EDNT)*

> *14. Remind them of these things, solemnly witnessing before God not to fight with words, for they are not useful but bring destruction to the ones hearing. 15.* **Be eager to present yourself approved to God, a workman unashamed, cutting straight the word of truth. 16. But avoid blasphemous and worthless chatter: for they will cause more disobeying of the Word.** *(2 Timothy 2:14-16 EDNT)*

A mature witness in the city square or market place is one who lives a life in contrast to others and transacts business with a Messiah-like attitude. They have a predisposition to behave honestly and fairly toward others regardless of the situation. This does not come naturally; it comes with maturity, experience, good instruction, and the prompt of the Holy Spirit. In Acts 11, Barnabas and Paul taught the new converts in Antioch for "*one whole year*" or daily and those who became active in the public square and marketplace using what they were taught.

As the believers began to transact their affairs in the market place as honest and professional individuals, the public recognized their lifestyle behavior as Messiah-like. (Acts 11:26) It was truly a lifestyle in contrast to contemporaries and later became a mark of identification as a follower of Christ. It was not the church who recognized these learners, but the people in the public square and marketplace who saw the difference in their lifestyle and behavior. Also, the public in Acts 4:13-22, confessed that the fearlessness and fluency of speech of Peter and John was attributed to being companions of Jesus. Faith-based relationships can make a difference in the public square.

> *36. Be compassionate, as your Father is also merciful and forgiving. 37. Do not pass judgment,* **release others from blame, and you shall not be condemned**.
>
> (Luke 6:36 EDNT)
>
> *19. Wherefore, my cherished band of believers: because of the righteousness of God, let everyone be ready listeners, slow to express our mind, slow to take offence: 20. for anger does not bear fruit acceptable to God. 21.* **Wherefore put aside all moral corruption and the abundance of worthless behavior and receive with a teachable spirit the firmly established word, which is able to make safe that spiritual part of you that determines all behavior.** *(James 1:19-21 EDNT)*

Salvation is a personal matter between an individual and God with the assistance of a friend.

11

GENTLENESS and LONG-SUFFERING with the Lost

The line has been etched in the sands of time: there is a definable difference between a true follower of Jesus and those who choose to be an unbeliever. Christian discipleship deals with separation from old ties and an exclusive attachment to Jesus. Yet, the Word provides explicit guidance for the believer to reach out to the unconverted. It begins with the natural impulse to share any enjoyable experience with another and continues with *"as you go into all the world, make disciples."* This strongly suggests that evangelism and

> Personal viewpoints and values are major factors that impact the daily struggle of leaders and managers. This is true in all aspects of life, but especially true at the workplace. Most organized enterprises today talk about good business to guide the required effort to achieve a profitable outcome. However, saying the right words is the easy part; doing the work to make the words happen is the struggle. This is where faith-based principles and values influence the decision and behavior process in organizational output.

the guidance and teaching to make a convert into a learner is a responsibility of every mature believer, not only the work of the established church. In fact, the challenge of Jesus to His followers (Matthew 28:16-20) was clearly given to individual and close followers of Jesus even before the church was established at Pentecost.

A primary reason of a believer's walk with God is to share His love with others. Individuals are *"saved to serve"* and share their faith with others. A compelling missional attitude of believers is expressed in these words of an unknown poet:

> *Can we whose souls are lighted*
> *With wisdom from on high;*
> *Can we to souls benighted*
> *The lamp of life deny?*

Believers must be a light to the unsaved, who should be reached in the public square and the marketplace where they daily gather. Simply inviting the lost to *"come to church"* is a human avoidance of spiritual responsibility. Each believer has an obligation to witness at each opportunity to anyone who will listen. To fail to share is a spiritual weakness.

When an individual reaches the sanctuary of a place of worship unconverted, it is evidence the New Testament evangelism is not adequately working. Lost souls must be reached at the *"earliest point in time, at the farthest distance from a place of worship."* The lost must be reached where they live and work. There is no reference in scripture that tells a lost person to seek out a church, listen to music they do not understand, hear a sermon that tells them they are on their way to hell, and present themselves before a crowd and bear their soul in public. Salvation is a personal matter between an individual and God with the assistance of a friend.

In old England, when William Booth started the Salvation Army (1865), *he was criticized by the Church of England for his unorthodox approach to reach the lost. His response, "You ring your church bells which say, "Come to church, Come to church" but nobody comes; we go to the streets and beat the base drum that says,* **"Fetch'um, fetch'um, and we get 'um!"**

For God has not given us the spirit of cowardice, but of power and of love and self-control.

(2 Timothy 1:7 EDNT)

A believer may not appreciate the lifestyle behavior of the unconverted, but the gentleness and long-suffering with the lost starts with where they are at the moment. Long-suffering is literally, *"love all stretched out" and includes patience, forgiveness, tolerance, and accommodation until spiritual change comes.* Believers may *"hate the sin"* but must "love the sinner." Since believers are to *"love their enemies and pray for those who despitefully* use them," it is a given that believers can do no less for lost souls. In both references to the Golden Rule (Matthew 5; Luke 6) it is tied to enemies. Should believer do less for the lost?

The lost must be met where they are and as they are. Scripture never requires the lost to leave their culture or language to hear the Good News. The old idea that *"individuals must be cleaned up before they can be saved and in that order"* has proved to be ineffective. In fact, as believers mature in true discipleship they are often separated from those who need mercy and saving grace.

The light of gathered believers may shine inside the sanctuary on Sunday, but the lost are not there. True converts are to be healing salt and beneficial light to the lost outside the four walls in the darkness of an evil world. Believers must shine their light where it can do the most good. Inviting a friend to a home setting with other believes may be good place to start when one is unresponsive to personal witness. The first step after prayer for a lost friend is to find a way to associate them with a small group of committed believers meeting regularly for prayer and discussions about family, relationships, and spiritual matters that affect the individual. Such a cell group is a good place to turn a friends into a believer. Such exposure to several believers and being able to speak freely often opens the door for the cure of souls and the winning of the lost. Then the converts may be brought to the sanctuary for baptism, membership in a larger fellowship and discipleship training.

Various individuals are at different levels of awareness and bringing an individual into contact with several believers at once may cause a mature openness to spiritual matters. Engels Scale of Awareness has been reversed here as an intervention strategy to assist in moving individuals toward acceptance of grace and forgiveness by a loving God. The unconverted must be gently moved through the initial awareness of need to the decision to repent and accept God's love and forgiveness.

	AWARENESS	**Countdown**
•	Awareness of Supreme Being	-10
•	No Effective Knowledge of Christianity	-9
	UNCONVERTED POOL	
•	Initial Awareness of Need	-8
•	Interest—Acceptance of Medium	-7

_____PERSONAL AWARENESS
- Awareness of Gospel -------------------------- -6
- Grasp of Implications -------------------------- -5

_____REALIZATION OF NEED
- Positive Attitude---------------------------------- -4
- Personal Problem Recognition----------------- -3

_____DECISION TO ACT
- Challenge/Decision to Act----------------------- **-2**

_____ENCOUNTER
- *Repentance/Faith in Christ* --------------------- **-1**

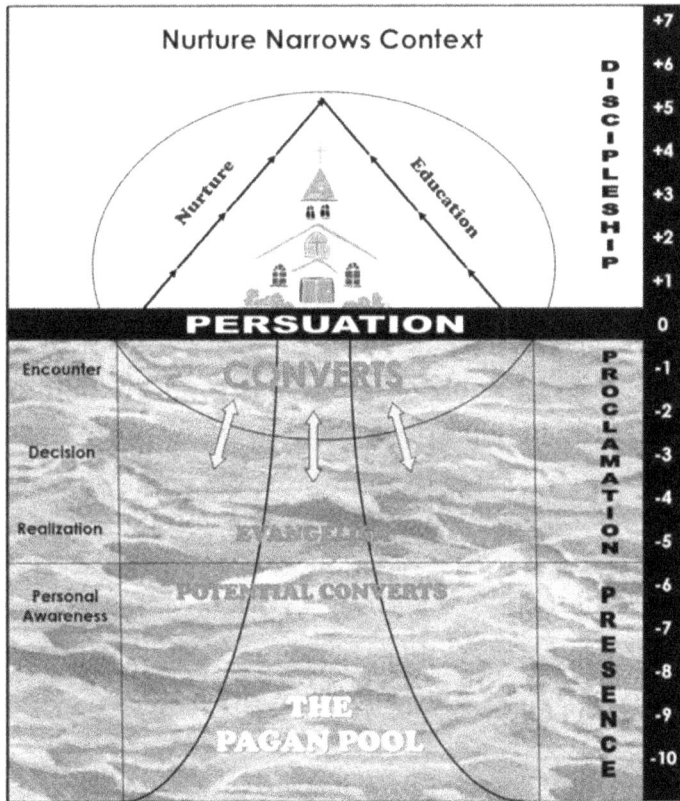

Modified Engel's Scale—this modified Engel's scale must be understood to assure adequate communication with the unconverted.

Study the Modified Engel's Scale above to better understand the necessary steps to bring the message of saving grace to the lost. Please notice the countdown process that brings individuals to a Decision to Act and Repentance at minus **2** and **1**. When this is attempted earlier, it is premature and usually fails.

Periods of awareness and intervention by Christians are required prior to a direct encounter that may or may not lead to a conversion experience.. The periods are:

1. Awareness (10-6)
2. Realization (5)
3. A Period of Decision (4-2)
4. Encounter (1)

Intervention strategies take three forms:

a. A Ministry of Presence (10-6)

b. A Period of Proclamation (5-2)

c. A Time of Persuasion (1)

Once an Encounter is made during the time of persuasion, the individuals involved must make a firm decision. This decision begins a Period of Incorporation. Converts must be nourished and nurtured through Discipleship Training into the active life of a believer. Several steps are evident:

1. Post-decision Evaluation
2. Incorporation
3. Personal Fruitfulness
4. Conceptual Growth
5. Discovery of Spiritual Gifts
6. Incarnational (Social) Growth

7. Stewardship
8. Prayer
9. Use of Spiritual Gifts
10. Witness-Reproduction

The Period of Incorporation requires the Christian community to assist the convert in learning to follow Christ. These steps are:

a. Discipleship

b. Christian Education

c. Body Life

d. *Koinonia* (fellowship)

e. *Diakonia* (service)

Christian love is confirmed by loving the unlovable; however, loving an enemy does not mean that the wrong is condoned or that sinful conduct is approved. Life is too short to permit holding a grudge, seeking revenge, or showing a spiteful or hateful spirit. This brings more hurt and depresses the mind and robs life of true happiness. While a forgiving spirit gives joy, peace and a deep satisfaction that forgiveness was the right thing to do in each situation, every time and every place it happens. It should be remembered that meekness is not weakness, but a *"teachable spirit"* toward others and is entirely consistent with constructive faith-based behavior.

Treating others as one wishes to be treated is not only a golden rule, it is a manifestation of the spirit of Jesus and Stephen and many others that could be lifted from the pages of history. Forgiving enables a believer to maintain a positive and prayerful attitude toward even wrongdoers. Believers must show the positive virtues of love, mercy, and forgiveness as taught by Jesus and practiced by His early followers recorded in scripture and church history. Evil must be overcome with good. This is a vital part of a faith-based lifestyle. Reconciliation is the true objective of forgiveness and a primary benefit to the individuals involved and the whole band of believers.

> *19. My band of believers, if any of you do stray from the true path, and one turn you about. 20.* **let the brother know, that he who turns one back from the error of his way into the right path, covers many faults and makes him safe, restoring his usefulness to the congregation.** *(James 5:19-20 EDNT)*

12

LOVE and FORGIVENESS for Enemies

BETTER TO BE SLAPPED WITH THE TRUTH
THAN KISSED WITH A LIE.

(Russian translation of Proverbs 27:6)

The Latin construct of *compassion* is one of those "*together with*" words with deep and significant meaning. There is an element of *patience* meaning *to remain under the pressure of a situation until relief can be given.* [A Rolaids will not provide the needed relief.] *Forgiveness* is related to *compassion* and is *a sharing of the suffering and distress of another* **together with** *a desire to alleviate both the symptoms and the causes of the sorrow and anguish of the afflicted one.*

> 35. But love your enemies and lend without expecting a return; and your reward shall be great; and you shall be the children of the Highest: for He is kind to the unthankful and to the evil. 36. Be compassionate, as your Father is also merciful and forgiving. 37. Do not pass judgment, release others from blame, and you shall not be condemned. 38. Give and others will press gifts into the pockets of your garment and good measure will be yours. For the same standard you use in giving shall be used to measure gifts to you. (Luke 6:35-38 EDNT)

Believers must understand that God's love placed in their heart by the Holy Spirit is stronger than hate and must never be denied or expressed only in human terms: obedience is commanded, *"Love your enemies. Pray for those who despitefully use you."* Believers must exercise absolute obedience to the words of Jesus. There is no route or comfortable retreat to the Old Testament ethics which condoned something less than redeeming love for enemies. (Matthew 5:43-44 and Leviticus 19:18ff)

A general law of the Kingdom is to *"Love your enemies,"* this love is *agape* or one-way love, the way God loves all mankind; not a selected affection for those to whom one is attracted by appearance or personality. Forgiveness is the intentional and deliberate process by which an individual undergoes a change of attitude and feeling regarding an offender and releases all negative emotions and renounces any vengefulness against the individual.

Why? First, because God demands it; second, because the enemy is a human soul suffering from a lack of maturity and under the stress of wrong-doing. Oh! for goodness sake, can an enemy really be loved by God and by redeemed believers within their circle of contacts? What about those harmed by the enemy's action? Looking at the example of Jesus, Stephen, and the martyrs of church history. What about the Golden Rule? Under the similar circumstances, how would you want to be treated? This enemy is some parent's lost child in need of love and forgiving mercy from God and other members of the human race. It is important to note that both references to the Golden Rule (Matthew 5; Luke 6) are tied to enemies.

Forgiveness is significantly different from condoning or excusing someone for misdeeds; it is an act of love expressed to a broken person for whom Jesus died and for whom someone else cares enough to share in their suffering and assist in their restoration to wholeness. It may be impossible to restore an enemy to full physical and legal position of safety, but it is possible the person can be redeemed and have a place in heaven.

Forgiveness has a spiritual element that causes one to act unilaterally and forgive not to remember the offense against the offender. In sacred scripture (Mark 9:42; 11:24-26)) clearly the deeper meaning of "offend" includes *"cause to stumble or entice to sin."* This is part of the spirituality embeddedness in forgiveness and requires a spark of divinity commonly expressed in the statement *"to err is human, but to forgive is divine."* Scripture is clear, if one does not forgive an offense; they become guilty before God as an offender themselves. The holding on to a grudge or malice brings painful sorry to a stubborn will and bitterness to the human spirit. Full redemption and vindication comes only from God.

> *That is why I say, Whatever you desire, when you pray, believe that you receive it, and you will have it.* <u>*25. And when you stand up to pray, forgive anything you are holding against anyone: so that your Father in heaven may forgive you your moral wrongs.*</u> **26. But if you do not forgive, neither will your Father who is in heaven forgive your transgressions.** *(Mark 11:24-26)*

Forgiveness is not just forgetting by removing awareness of the offense; it is more than pardoning or exonerating an offender of wrongdoing. A genuine act of forgiveness is permit pray and the Word to *"blot out the memory"* of the offense and through grace and maturity behave as if it never happened. This is what regeneration is to the believer. Provided an offender accepts forgiveness and reconciliation that are restored and rejuvenated and *"in Christ all things have become new."* This is both maturity at work and the godly aspects to forgiveness working toward a renaissance for the offender.

When this happens, God has forgiven and does not remember any transgression against the offender the offended must do the same. To say "*I forgive"* is the mature part, but to be able to treat the situation as if it never happened is the spiritual part of reconciliation that takes place with a divine work in the heart of both the offended and the offender. God must have a special **Angel SWAT Team** that work exclusively on this issue for all concerned. This process is supported through prayer, the Word and loving friends. Ephesians 5:26,27 speaks of Christ consecrating and purifying believers with *"the cleansing water of the word."*

> *17. Therefore if any man be in Christ, he is a new creation: observe, the old things have passed away; all things have become new. 18. All things are of God, who has brought us together in us the ministry of bringing people together; 19. how that God was in Christ bringing together the world to Himself, not counting their false steps and blunders against them; and has committed us to speak intelligent words that bring man and God together. 20. Now seeing we are representatives for Christ, as though God did make His appeal through us: we implore you in Christ's stead, come together with God.* (2 Corinthians 5:17-20 EDNT).

Traveling down a one-way street can be confusing and dangerous when others do not obey the rules of the road; i.e. *"don't impede the flow of traffic and always travel with the traffic flow, etc."* The sender must adequately communicate a willingness to forgive and the receiver must acknowledge and accept the forgiveness: otherwise the static of the situation will hinder the transfer of true meaning and there will be a failure of communication.

Forgiving can have a one-sided dimension when the offender does not acknowledge accountability and follow scriptural rules. The matter is not *"a game"* or a *"French comedy-drama"* or a *"sarcastic situation;"* it is a serious process required by God between mature adults. Those who fail to reconcile will retain accountability to God and their guilt in the matter. If associated in a faith-based group, the unreconciled will be held accountable for failure to resolve the issue and from a for unrestored fellowship with the forgiver. Unresolved culpability will fester and eventually without reconciliation, punishment will come from a faith-based fellowship or directly from God. When reconciliation fails, there will be collateral damage to family, friends and the whole group will suffer loss. Regardless of the offender's attitude, the forgiver stands forgiven in the eyes of God. Yet, the breach remains an open and active. This is not a good place to be, because those who fail to accept a genuine declaration of forgiveness are to be treated as an unbeliever. Now, the issue becomes their salvation, and this come only from God. Those who do not accept the work of reconciliation become under the injunction, *"Love your enemies, pray for those who despitefully use you."* These names move to the top the believer's prayer list!

> 5. This then is the message which we have heard of Him, and announce to you, that God is light, and no darkness can find a place in Him. 6. If we say that we have fellowship with Him, and at the same time walk in darkness, we lie, and are not living the truth: 7. but **if we walk in the light, as He is in the light, we have fellowship one with another, and the blood of Jesus Christ His Son cleanses us from all sin. 8.** If we say that we have no sin, we deceive ourselves, and the truth is not in us. 9. **If we admit our sins, faithful is He and righteous in order that He may cleanse us from all wickedness. 10. If we deny that we have sinned, it means that we are treating Him as a liar; and that His word does not dwell in our hearts.**(1 John 1:5-10 EDNT)

A believer may defend the faith, protect the family and life itself, but must never retaliate or seek personal revenge against an offender. Certainly, it is unnatural to love an enemy; such unrealistic behavior is in the spiritual sphere of *agape* (one-way) love. Such behavior comes from deep within a consecrated heart as an effort to follow the primary example of Jesus on the Cross: *"Father, forgive them, for they know not what they do."* It should be remembered that one who heard this declaration triumphantly accepted immediately his place in paradise and another tragically rejected the opportunity. Perhaps this assists believers not to be unduly disturbed when an offender continues to reject forgiveness. Yet, one soul is worth the whole world!

This forgiving love comes from an understanding that it is the sin nature that causes individuals to commit wrongful acts which offend others; therefore, the required action of the believer when faced with the "*need to forgive"* is to earnestly pray that the wrongdoer will be delivered from the ways of sin and brought into fellowship with God and man.

The stoning of Stephen is a perfect example (Acts 7:60) *"On his knees, he prayed with a loud voice, Lord fix no this sin against them."* The calmness and peace with which Stephen forgave and accepted his suffering clearly demonstrated the first real example of a missional lifestyle after the resurrection of Jesus. His quality of forgiveness spoke loudly to the young man Saul who was holding his clothing during and consenting to his death by stoning. Stephen's forgiving spirit ultimately influenced Saul who became Paul, the great Apostle to the Gentiles and was used by God to write one-fourth of the New Testament. The forgiving spirit of both Jesus and Stephen demonstrate the value of the process. Therefore, we should be willing to participate in sharing the message of grace and forgiveness even with enemies. Opportunities missed are openings to witness that are lost. Those who have experienced the love of God must not neglect or deny the sharing with anyone who will listen.

The Chorus lyrics of an old hymn, "*You Never mentioned Him to Me* "(James Rowe, 1949) speaks clearly to this issue:

> *"You never mentioned Him to me,*
> *You helped me not the light to see;*
> *You met me day by day and knew I was astray,*
> *Yet never mentioned Him to me!"*

Life is filled with difficult relationships and circumstances where you will have people to forgive, and with whom you need to reconcile.

AfterWords
by First Readers

"...to forgive is divine!"

Forgiveness is not only the "sunrise of reconciliation" it is also the glue that holds all relationships together. In choosing this central principle of Christianity, Dr. Green addressed twelve aspects of forgiveness that lead to spiritual growth and maturity. A propositional statement in the Preface sets the tone of the book: "Forgiveness is the sunrise of reconciliation. The power to forgive the wrongdoings of others is an apparent capability divinely furnished believers as a tool to assist the maturation of individuals and harmony among family, friends and associates."

With God's extravagant forgiveness as an artesian well, forgiveness is core to worship, interpersonal relationships on all levels including marriage, family, neighbors, community, work, and reaching others with the love of God in Christ. Dr. Green exegetes the Great Commission of Matthew 28:19-29 clarifying the use of the participles and providing the historical rationale why "go" was used by King James scholars rather than "going". An interesting diagram of Engels Scale of Awareness illustrates the levels of engagement with those who have not come to faith. The book climaxes with forgiving when wronged. Jesus demonstrated this on the cross and

Stephen echoed the same at the beginning of the church. Forgiving when wronged is a vital and Spirit-empowered behavior. It is not possible to go through life without being wronged and hurt by others. How one responds is crucial to their spiritual growth.

I have personally travelled the road of forgiveness, professionally and personally. I highly commend this book to all believers and especially those called to teach and lead the church.

—**Roy C. Price, DMin, DPhil, Pastor/Missionary**

We cannot have the right relationship with Jesus without a forgiving heart. When we accept Christ we accept the responsibility to forgive and we are blessed with the capacity. But this ability must be nourished and studying the precepts Dr. Green identifies in this book under the guidance of the Holy Spirit will increase our ability to forgive and also to see our own faults.

—**Jerry Fleming, DPhil, Businessman**

I am interested in your new book on forgiveness; could you do some teaching out of this new book? Not really calling it a conference, but more in the way an introduction into the subject matter you cover in your book. My thought is that through 2020, we can cover some of the most important aspects of this major work. I still believe this may be "the book" that will prove to be a most timely approach to what the Church needs most.

—**Bill Christian, PhD, Senior Pastor, New Life Church**

About The Author

Hollis L. Green, ThD, PhD, DLitt, is a Clergy-Educator with public relations and business credentials and  doctorates in theology, philosophy, and education. A Distinguished Professor of Education and Social Change at the graduate level for over three decades, Dr. Green is a Diplomate in the Oxford Society of Scholars, and author of 50+ books and numerous articles. He served six years as a member of the U.S. Senate Business Advisory Board and with certified membership in several public relations societies (RPRC, PRSA, and IPRC). He served pastorates in five states, was a Military Chaplain during the Vietnam era, a denominational official for 18 years, and traveled in ministry and lectured in over 100 countries.

Dr. Green was the founder (1974) A.I.D. Ltd., Associated Institutional Developers, Ltd. (an international Public Relations and Corporate Consultant Company). He was Vice-President (1974-1979) of Luther Rice Seminary (www.lru.edu) and became the founding President (1981) and Chancellor (1991-2008) of Oxford Graduate School, [www.ogs.edu]. As part of a global outreach, Dr. Green

founded OASIS UNIVERSITY (2002) in Trinidad, West Indies. [www.oasisgradedu.org] where he continues to serve as a Distinguished Professor of Education and Social Change and Chancellor. In 2004, he assisted in establishing Greenleaf Educational Foundation in Colorado to advance educational issues.

In addition to other endeavors, Dr. Green launched Global Educational Advance, Inc. and GEA Press (2007) [www.gea-books.com] to advance higher education and positive social change through publishing, curriculum advance, library/learning resources, improved instruction, and global book distribution with 30,000 distributors in 100 countries. His books and assisting authors in publishing are a logical outgrowth of a sixty-year ministry through education. He serves Global as Corporate Chair and Co-publisher with his sons, Barton and Brian. Dr. Green continues to travel, speak, teach, write books and work with authors in publishing their creative work.

Appendix A

An Obituary for Common Sense

(The London Times)

Today we mourn the passing of a beloved old friend, Common Sense, who has been with us for many years. No one knows for sure how old he was, since his birth records were long ago lost in bureaucratic red tape. He will be remembered as having cultivated such valuable lessons as:

- - Knowing when to come in out of the rain;
- - Why the early bird gets the worm;
- - Life isn't always fair; and
- - Maybe it was my fault.

Common Sense lived by simple, sound financial policies (don't spend more than you can earn) and reliable strategies (adults, not children, are in charge).

His health began to deteriorate rapidly when well-intentioned but overbearing regulations were set in place. Reports of a 6-year-old boy charged with sexual harassment for kissing a classmate; teens suspended from school for using mouthwash after lunch; and a teacher fired for reprimanding an unruly student, only worsened his condition.

Common Sense lost ground when parents attacked teachers for doing the job that they themselves had failed to do in disciplining their unruly children. It declined even further when schools were required to get parental consent to administer sun lotion or an aspirin to a student; but could not inform parents when a student became pregnant and wanted to have an abortion.

Common Sense lost the will to live as the churches became businesses; and criminals received better treatment than their victims.

Common Sense took a beating when you couldn't defend yourself from a burglar in your own home and the burglar could sue you for assault.

Common Sense finally gave up the will to live, after a woman failed to realize that a steaming cup of coffee was hot. She spilled a little in her lap, and was promptly awarded a huge settlement.

Common Sense was preceded in death,
- - by his parents, Truth and Trust,
- - by his wife, Discretion,
- - by his daughter, Responsibility,
- - and by his son, Reason.

He is survived by his 5 stepbrothers;
- - I Know My Rights
- - Then - Someone Else Is To Blame
- - I'm A Victim
- Pay me for Doing Nothing

Not many attended his funeral because, so few realized he was gone!

Source: (Spiritual/Scientific Teachers)

https://www.facebook.com/groups/367827133264840/permalink/2505147666199432/?sfnsn=mo

Appendix B

Theology of the Sweat Cloth

It was assumed that the basis for providing man a helpmate was to protect the family from immorality and provide a secure place for the birth and education of children. The common objective is for children to become moral citizens of the world and ultimately a mystical citizen of a heaven.

Since God established the edict concerning work (Genesis 3:19). This decree was for the whole of life until the grave. Perhaps present-day believers should be reminded that God's injunction that *"mankind would earn their bread by the sweat of work"* has not been rescinded. Also, Paul's command to the Believers at Thessalonica has not been annulled: **"No work—no eat!"**

> *10. When we were with you we instructed you that if any would not work, neither should they eat. 11. For we understand that some among you behave in an undisciplined manner refusing to work at all, but interfere in other's affairs. 12. Now with the authority of the Lord Jesus Christ, we urge such people to attend quietly to their own affairs and earn their own bread.*
> (2 Thessalonians 3:10-12 EDNT)

Paul made clear that God's declaration about work had a theological application to the individual's faith and family,

8. If anyone provides not for his own people, and especially his family, he has denied the faith, and is worse than an unbeliever. (1 Timothy 5:8 EDNT)

The gospel writer Luke (19:20-28) shared a story where Jesus expressed grave concern for a man who had funds but did no use them properly. It seems idle servant wrapped his money in a "sweat cloth" for safe keeping. It has been noted that the idle man did not need a sweat cloth for its proper use (Genesis 3:19) but instead used his "sweat cloth" as a security wrapping to store his money. This did not please Jesus! The construct of the "sweat cloth, napkin, or handkerchief" was found in an early papyrus marriage contract as part of the dowry. Since the cloth was for a working man, the father of the bride would pass to the new husband a "sweat cloth" signifying "*I have worked and supported this my daughter from birth until now; that responsibility is now on your shoulders.*" The clear message "*Go to work and support my daughter and her children; they are a part of my extended family and essential to my legacy.*" A true legacy cannot be established without hard work… cooperation and a "sweat cloth" will be needed!

A good example is at the Resurrection of Jesus when John and Peter ran to the Tomb in the Garden. They found the grave clothes of Jesus that had been hardened with oil and spices still in the form of a man, but the napkin or "sweat cloth" that covered the open place at the face was removed, folded neatly and laid aside. Why? Peter could see into the grave clothes and know the Jesus had been raised, but the "sweat cloth" as a symbol of hard work was **"folded and placed separately"** to send a message to Peter. *"As* *the Father sent me, so send I you! I have finished my work and will return to My Father. It is now your time to take up the task and do the hard labor to advance the Kingdom,."* The task of reaching the lost and making disciples had been sublet to Peter, the Apostles, and to all who followed Jesus. That was expressed in the general Challenge to His Followers after the Resurrection (Matthew 28:19,20)

> v..19 Consider the only imperative of the verse translated "teach." The Greek word means to instruct with the purpose of making a disciple; the word suggested not only to learn but to be attached to and a follower of a teacher. Greek words have special designations, **matheteuo** (teach) here was classified as **aorist imperative active** which denotes a command, or entreaty and indicates the action as being accomplished by the subject of the verb. Later versions translated the word as "make disciples" which was better. A basic problem relates to the three participles: Going [going or as you go] ... baptizing ... teaching are participles dependent upon the main verb "teach" translated "make disciples." Although such a construction is not uncommon for the participles themselves to assume the force of a weak imperative, it is indirect similar to the indirect command in modern English, i.e. "As you go, close the door!" However, the command "to make disciples" is the primary command, while the participles (weak commands) going, baptizing and teaching are ways of fulfilling the primary command. Early translators the first one the strength of a "direct command" rather than a simple   .

A PURE HEART
IS THE BEGINNING
OF SERVICE TO OTHERS!

Appendix C

The "Together-Strong" NETWORK

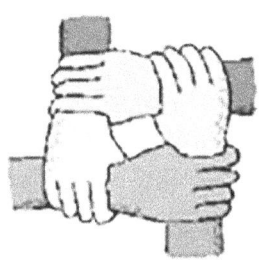

TOGETHER-STRONG NETWORK

A strategy to organize men to participate in the work of the congregation based on James 1:27

The ancient Greeks, in whose language God gave us the New Testament, discovered that if a person really cared about the circumstances of others, he might enter vicariously into that person's experience. They called this *sympathos*, meaning "with suffering," from which comes the English word "sympathy." By means of sympathy, one enters into the minds and hearts of those who struggle or suffer, to share their burdens. The early followers of Christ discovered that when sympathy was sincere, a miracle resulted among the supported. They called it *confortis*, meaning **"together strong."** and from it came the present word, "comfort." This is the basis for the name: **"Together-Strong" NETWORK.**

The time has come to organize the men of the congregation into a **"Together-Strong" NETWORK** to assist the ministerial leadership with the necessary services to maintain both personal and spiritual growth of the families. It is for this reason that a "TOGETHER-STRONG" NETWORK has become a strategy to organize the men to participate in the work of the congregation. All men who regularly participate in the worship services, programs, and activities of the congregation are NETWORK. The men will be organized into groups or squads based on their location, shift work, trade skills and availability. The writings of James should serve as a guide to the men. In particular James 1:27 *Free from all that would dim the transparency in belief and conduct before God and the Father is this, to go see and relieve the orphans without a father's protection and the women lacking a husband in their distress, and to keep himself untainted with guilt.*

Leadership will identify the needs of widows, women alone, the sick or needy and issue a written work order. For example, a widow's roof leaks, a single mother has difficulty with raising a young son, a family needs assistance with transportation, etc.' The NETWORK squad nearest the need or the one best equipped will receive the "work order" and follow-up with the assistance of others. A good orientation to "faith and deeds" is found in James 2:14-26

> *14. What is the benefit, my cherished band of believers, if a man says he has faith, and have not deeds? Can faith save him? 15. If a brother or sister is destitute of daily necessities and has no clothing, 16. of what use is it to say to the needy, Come in and be warmed, eat all you can and depart in peace; although you give them none of the essentials which are needful to the body? 17. Even so faith without*

praiseworthy deeds, is like an unburied corpse left alone. 18. Yes, a man may affirm that he has faith, and not have deeds; show me faith apart from deeds, and I will show you faith by means of my deeds.

Early Christians, when they witnessed the struggle or suffering of colleagues, acted to express their common feelings with "their fellows." This is precisely why the NETWORK was established. We must build a stronger relationship with godly people who will assist with spiritual accountability to accomplish achievable things. The early believers seemed to have an understanding of mutual and parallel susceptibility to evil conditions that prevailed. As early Christians expressed their concern for one another, they created the first **together-strong network**. This is what the men of the congregation need as an ongoing program. Will you be a part of this ministry?

- - - - -- -- -- -- -- -- -- -- -- -

YES, I will be a part of the "TOGETHER-STRONG" NETWORK

NAME_____

Address _____

City_____State_____

ZIP _____

Home Telephone (   )_____

Cell/mobile (   )_____

Pager_____

E-mail:_____

I work ( ) first shift;( ) second shift; ( ) third shift; ( ) Mon-Fri; ( ) week-ends. My days off _____;
Best time of day available for NETWORK responsibility; _____AM; _____PM. My work experience and areas of interest are: [ ] A prayer partner; [ ] Auto mechanic skills; [ ] Carpenter skills; [ ] Counseling skills; [ ] Electrician skills; [ ] House painter; [ ] Lawn and garden work; [ ] music; [ ] plumber; [ ] roofer; [ ] list other interests:

_____
_____
_____
_____
_____

With this information, the needs of widows and orphans can be placed on a "WORK ORDER" and assigned to the proper person for prompt completion.

Appendix D

Wound Wash

Everyone has wounds. Most wounds, hurts, or offenses come from a loved one, a close friend, or a colleague. Those whom you love can hurt you the most, even a friend can offend; however, simple "*forgiveness*" is the secret to cleansing the wound and removing the hurt and stain.

*Time doesn't heal anything...
it only teaches us
to live with the pain.
Yet, there is a sacred path
to heal wounds and bring
true reconciliation --
walking that path can
remove both pain and stain.*

Follow these seven steps:

"Consecrate and purify it with the cleansing Water of the Word..." (Ephesians 5:26 EDNT)

1. **Before starting the Wound Wash** process, pray a simple prayer to clear your mind. Try a silent prayer or a calm period of meditation to seek assistance of Providence. Limit your exposure to background noise. Traffic or ringing phones can dampen your mood. If nothing else works, try ear plugs for a short periods to limit the noise.

A HEALING PRAYER

LORD, I COME TO YOU WITH MY BURDENED HEART,
ALLOW YOUR HEALING HAND TO TOUCH ME.
HEAL MY SOUL WITH YOUR COMPASSION.
TOUCH MY SPIRIT WITH YOUR COURAGE.

FILL MY MIND WITH YOUR WISDOM
AND
MY MOUTH WITH WORDS OF KINDNESS.
TEACH ME TO REACH OUT TO OTHERS.
HELP ME IMPROVE MY EXAMPLE TO OTHERS.

MAY YOUR LOVING HEART BRING HEALTH TO MY
BODY AND SPIRIT
THAT I MAY SERVE YOU WITH MY STRENGTH.

TOUCH GENTLY THIS LIFE YOU CREATED
AND GIVE ME A FORGIVING SPIRIT
FOR NOW, AND EACH TIME IT IS NEEDED.

AMEN!

2. **Then, forgive the one who caused the wound**; including yourself if you had a part in the process.

3. **Now, read** and be influenced by the Spirit

15. Look carefully how you walk, not foolishly, but in the light, 16. buying up every opportunity, because these are evil days. 17. Wherefore be not reckless, but prudently understand the will of the Lord. 18. Stop excessively drinking wine, which influences riotous living; more willingly be influenced by the Spirit; 19. but speak to one another in exalted verse, songs of praise, and sacred music, singing and making melody with the music of your hearts, to the Lord; 20. continue giving thanks to God the Father for all things in the name of our Lord Jesus Christ; 21. line up under one another in reverence to Christ. 22. Wives, line up under and adapt to your own husbands, as unto the Lord. 23. For the husband is in charge of the wife, even as Christ is in charge of the church: and He is the champion of the church. 24. Therefore as the church is to line up under the authority of Christ, so let the wives line up under their husbands in all things.

25. Husbands, be devoted to your wives, even as Christ is devoted to the church, and gave Himself for it; 26. that he might consecrate and purify it with the cleansing water of the word, 27. that he might present the church to himself as a glorious bride, without spot, wrinkle or blemish. 28. So must men love their wives as if they were their own body. He who loves his wife loves himself. 29. For no man ever loathed his own body; but nourishes and values it, even as the Lord values the church: 30. for we are members of his body. 31. For this reason shall a man leave his father and mother and cleave intimately to his wife, and they shall become one new body.* 32. This is a great sacred secret: but I speak concerning Christ and the church. 33. Nevertheless let each one in particular love his wife even as himself; and the wife should look to and pay attention to her husband. (Ephesians 5:15-33 EDNT)

---

*v31 A new body or "one flesh" is sarx which suggests a human body apart from the soul. Probably this is the bonding that comes with the first child and not only the emotional bonding of a couple when vows are physically consummate

4. **Apply the cleansing power of forgiveness directly** on the wounded area of your life.

5. **Flush the wounded area freely** with fresh prayer and thanksgiving for God's forgiveness and the better things in life.

6. **Now, read** 1 Peter 4:7-11 EDNT.

7. The end of all things is near: live wisely, and keep your senses awake to greet the times of prayer. 8. Above all embrace each other in love that is constant and intense: because love covers a multitude of sins. 9. Never begrudge the hospitality you show one another. 10. As each has received a gift from God, so let all use such gifts in the service of one another, as good stewards of God's multi-sided grace. 11. Should any man speak, let him speak words sent from God; if a man serves, let him do it with God-given ability: that God may be glorified in all things through Jesus Christ, to whom be praise and dominion for ever and ever. Amen.

7. **THE WOUND WASH process** may be applied as often as needed, each time with a little extra prayer. Stop complaining – start living!

Dr. David A. Anderson, the founder/senior pastor of Bridgeway Community Church, is considered a leading authority on reconciliation based on race, wealth, culture, and faith. His book, *Gracism: The Art of Inclusion,* provides a Christian alternative to secular affirmative action through the Tenets of Gracism. These precepts may be used in the process of reconciliation at all levels of forgiveness, integration and building bridges for inclusion. It was my privileged to participate in both personal and corporate sessions where Dr. Anderson's principles of Gracism were repeated to each other; *to wit:*

I will lift you up,
I will share with you,
I will stand with you,

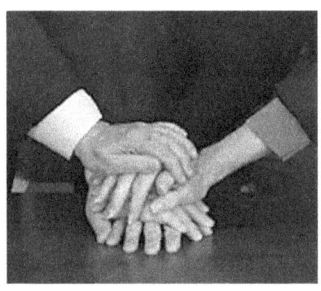

I will consider you,
I will celebrate with you,
I will cover you,
I will honor you.

The power in forgiveness is the divine enablement which provides believers the capacity to examine themselves, correct their part in any dispute, and forgive and restore good relations with others.

Appendix E

The Power Series

As developed, titles may be prioritized. May be sold as individual books or as a series. May be 7, 14, or 21 arranged in three Collections with 7 books in each. With God's assistance and reasonable health, I will complete this series in the next 3 to 5 years. God bless you and thank you for your prayerful support.

♦

I. **Power of Forgiveness and Reconciliation** (12/5/2019)
- Approval and Readiness in Spiritual Growth
- Respect and Forgiveness of Self and Others
- Affection and Togetherness in the Family
- Attitude and Action in Missional Lifestyle
- Peace and Harmony during the Collect
- Prayer and Renunciation in Confession
- Examination and Solidarity at Communion
- Togetherness and Faithfulness in Worship
- Transparency and Restoration with Believers
- Harmony and Witness in the Workplace
- Gentleness and Long-suffering with the Lost
- Love and Forgiveness for Enemies

II. **Power of Prayer and Perseverance**

III. **Power of Lordship and Worship**

IV. **Power of Giving and Receiving**

V. **Power of Lifestyle and Witness**

VI.	Power of Mission and Going
VII.	Power of Fellowship and Friends

♦

VIII.	Power of Assimilation and Application
IX.	Power of Learning and Sharing
X.	Power of Planting and Harvest
XI.	Power of Hunger and Pursuit
XII.	Power of Longevity and Legacy
XIII.	Power of Enthusiasm and Affirmation
XIV.	Power of Camaraderie and Companions

♦

XV.	Power of Hearth and Home
XVI.	Power of Confession and Communion
XVII.	Power of Purpose and Timetable
XVIII.	Power of Faith and Moral Excellence
XIX.	Power Scarcity and Abundance
XX.	Power of Connectivity and Friendship
XXI.	Power of Love and Hate

Appendix F

Steps to Spiritual Guidance

STEP ONE: Preparation and Fruitfulness
   Scriptural background: Ezekiel 36:26-32

1. God prepares His people for the work. (26)
2. God empowers His people for the walk. (2)
3. God Provides His people a Place. (28)
4. God preserves His people from sin. (29)
5. God multiplies the Harvest. (30
6. God causes His people to remember .(31)
7. God blesses His people for His sake. (32)

STEP TWO: Patience and Guidance
   Scriptural background: Isaiah 30:18-21

1. God is just; He will do right.(18)
2. Wait patiently and be blessed. (18)
3. Dwell in the land and weep no more. (19)
4. G190od hears your prayers. (19)
5. Adversity and affliction will teach you. (20)
6. Guidance will come if you go the wrong way. (21)
7. No guidance means you are on course. (21)

STEP THREE: Teamwork and Relationships

Scriptural background: 1 Peter 3:8-18

1. Do not attempt God's work alone; it is teamwork, a group effort. (8)
2. Be united in spirit, sympathizing with one another as family Be tenderhearted and humble. (8)
3. Do not retaliate, but bless others regardless of their attitude or actions. (9)
4. Bless others by praying for their welfare, happiness and protection.
5. Keep control of your tongue and enjoy life. (10)
6. Turn from evil and do good, pursue peace and righteousness. The Lord is against those who practice evil, oppose, frustrate, and defeat God's work. (11-12)
7. God rewards those who suffer for doing good. (13-14); Give a logical answer and quietly reward those who suffer for being right.(Do what is right and have a clear conscience (15-18)

STEP FOUR   Singleness and Servanthood

Scriptural background: Philippians 3:3-17

1. Focus on one thing at a time until the work is finished. (13)
2. Forget the way things worked in the past. This is a new day. (13)
3. Press into the future with spiritual servanthood. (14)
4. The prize is the approval of Christ. (14)
5. The call is upward for the spiritual mature. (15)

Appendix F: Steps to Spiritual Guidance

6. Hold your ground but keep walking. (16)
7. Keep your eyes on God and those who follow Him. (17)

STEP FIVE: Rejoicing and Strength

Scriptural background: Psalms 21:1,2; 37:1-18

1. Rejoice in God's strength. (21:1)
2. God does not withhold blessings from a rejoicing heart. (21:2)
3. Do not measure accomplishments by others. (3;1-3)
4. Get excited about God. (37:4)
5. Commit the plan to God and rust Him each day (37:5,6)
6. Be still and patient wait for peace. (37;7-11
7. It is better to be on God's side. The plot of the wicked will be defeated.(37:12-18)

STEP SIX: Stewardship and Self-sufficiency

Scriptural background: Philippians 4:10-18

1. Donors want to support people, but must have an opportunity and be appreciated. (10)
2. All gifts, although used for programs, must be seen as advancing God's work through individuals not institutions. (11)
3. Individuals must develop a self-sufficiency and be satisfied with God's supply. (12)
4. Christ is the source and all support comes at His prompting.(13)

5. It is right for others to contribute to personal need of labors in the vineyard. (14)
6. Gifts from churches are few, it is individuals who support Kingdom work.(15,16)
7. Do not seek gifts, but blessings for the giver. (18)

STEP SEVEN: Treasure and Self-preservation

Scriptural background: Matthew 6:19-34

1. Lose the instinct for self-preservation and gain a full life in Christ. Do not store resources. Use all you receive for the work of God. (19)
2. Lay up treasures in heaven so your heart and vision will be fixed on God. See the end result – not the immediate benefits. (20-23)
3. Do not try to serve two masters, God and possessions. (24)
4. Stop being uneasy about life. God is concerned about you; He will care for you. (25-31
5. God knows your needs. (32)
6. Seek first the Kingdom within yourself. (33)
7. Do not worry about the future. God is sufficient for each day. Trust Him. (34))

Appendix G

AFFIRMATION OF THE MARRIAGE VOWS

We are met in the presence of God to affirm the marriage vows of JOHN and JANE. The husband is under obligation to protect his wife, to shield her from the rough storms of the world, to cling to her with unfaltering fidelity, to cherish her with unfailing affections, and to guard her happiness with unceasing vigilance. And the wife is under obligation to love and cherish her husband, to honor and sustain him, and to be true to him in all ways.

This love of which I speak is slow to lose patience--it looks for a way of being constructive. It is not possessive: it is neither anxious to impress nor does it cherish inflated ideas of its own importance. Love has good manners and does not pursue selfish advantage. It is not touchy. It does not compile statistics of evil or gloat over the wickedness of other people. On the contrary, it is glad with all good men when Truth prevails. Love knows no limit to its endurance, no end to its trust, no fading of its hope; it can outlast anything. It is, in fact, the one thing that still stands when all else has fallen. Each one is under obligation to fulfill the love ordained of God and recorded in I Corinthians 13:1-13 (EDNT)

> *1. Even if I could speak the languages of men and angels and not have love, I would become an echoing gong or a clanging cymbal. 2. Even if I have the gift of speaking forth God's word, and understand sacred secrets, and all knowledge; and though I have absolute faith and be able to move mountains, and have not love, I am nothing. 3. And though I distribute all I possess to provide for the poor, and though I seal my witness at a burning stake, and have not love, there is no benefit*

for me. 4. Love is longsuffering and sympathetic; love has no jealousy, love is not anxious to impress others, does not hold inflated ideas of self-importance,5. Has good manners, is not self-seeking, is never provoked, does not keep score of wrongs; 6. takes no pleasure in wrongdoing, but rejoices when truth is victorious; 7. There is no limit to endurance, love has endless faith and great expectations, there is no end to love's tolerance. 8. Love stands when all else disintegrates: but preaching, the use of unnaturally acquired languages and present and fragmentary knowledge will be rendered entirely idle. 9. For we presently speak based on limited knowledge. 10. But when Christ returns, then our limited function will become inoperative. 11. When I was a child, I spoke, understood, and reasoned as a child: but becoming a man, I outgrew childish ways. 12. At the present we see only blurred reflections in polished metal; but then face to face the blurred image will be gone and we will see ourselves as God sees us. (EDNT)

And now, if you, knowing of nothing either legal or moral to forbid your continued union in marriage, wish to reaffirm your vows and assume the full obligations marriage, **indicate that wish by joining your right hands**.

JOHN, do you now freely take, JANE, whose hand you hold to be your wedded wife, and solemnly promise and reaffirm your vows to her and pledge to loyally fulfill your obligations as her husband to protect her, honor her, love her, and cherish her in adversity as well as in prosperity and keep yourself unto her alone, so long as you both shall live? The man shall answer: *I will.*

JANE, do you freely reaffirm your marriage vows, and accept this man, JOHN, whose hand you hold to be your wedded husband and solemnly promise that you will be unto him a tender, loving, and true wife through sunshine and shadow alike, and be faithful to him as long as you both shall live? The woman will answer: *I will.*

Then shall they loose their hands: We read in an old story that when God made a covenant with Noah, He set a bow in the cloud as a token of remembrance, and said, "I will look upon it, that I may remember the everlasting covenant." From this we learn that it is well for us, when we enter into solemn agreement one with another, to set apart some reminder of what we have promised. As tokens of your marriage covenant, you have each selected a wedding ring.

Here the ring(s) shall be given to the minister:

A chosen wedding ring fittingly represents the valued ties that unite husband and wife. These rings, endless until broken by outside forces, are fit symbols of the unbroken partnership of marriage which should continue until broken by death. Let them be unto you constant reminders of your obligations to each other, and mute incentives to their fulfillment.

Forasmuch as the husband imparts to his wife his name and receives her into his care and keeping, I give you this ring. Put it upon the wedding finger of your companion, and say to her these words: I, JOHN, give this ring to you, JANE, and by this act declare, in the presence of these witnesses, that I reaffirm my marriage vows to you and take you to be my beloved wife; that I will be unto you a faithful husband until death shall part us.

Take the ring which you have selected, put it upon the wedding finger of your companion and say to him these words: I, JANE, give this ring to you, JOHN, and thus declare, in the presence of these witnesses that you are the husband of my choice, that I will be faithful to you until death shall part us.

As you both wear wedding rings, they become a symbol of the perfect circle of duty that makes you one. As you hope for happiness in your married life, I charge you to be true to the vows you have taken. With your marriage, you begin life under new conditions and with larger responsibilities; and it is only by faithfully performing the duties and fulfilling the obligations of this new relationship that true and lasting happiness can be found.

Since, JOHN and JANE have openly declared their wishes to reaffirm their marriage vows and continue their legal marriage and pledged love and fidelity each to the other, and have confirmed the same by the giving and receiving of a ring, I, as a Minister of the Gospel, pronounce that they continue to be Husband and Wife. (Torches, candles, or salt may be used here!)

Would you look at each other and repeat: Entreat me not to leave you or to return from following you; for where you go I will go, and where you lodge I will lodge; your people shall be my people, and your God my God (Ruth 1:16).

Let us pray: Almighty God, heavenly Father of mankind, whose nature is love: Look with favor upon this man and this woman who have taken fresh vows before you. Grant this to be more than an outward union, but rather the blending of hearts and spirits. Bless each with the inward qualities of loyalty, self-control, trust, cooperation, and forgiveness, that they may keep faithfully this holy covenant, and may live together all their days in true love and perfect peace, through Jesus Christ. The Lord bless you and keep you; the Lord make His face to shine upon you, and be gracious unto you; the Lord lift up His countenance upon you and give you peace. Amen.

JOHN and JANE you may now seal your love and commitment with a kiss! Ladies and gentlemen: May I introduce a new and refreshed Mr. and Mrs. JOHN DOE.

Appendix H

Relevant Books by the Author

To understand the problems of faith-based entities and individuals, extensive research was done during the past two decades. Meanwhile, my schedule was filled with academic administration, teaching, research and writing, but colleagues and friends have encouraged sequels to my best-known works. In the decade following retirement that prompt was followed and produced twenty (25+) books in addition to ten Children's Novellas. (See www.gea-books.com.bookstore) or anywhere good books are sold.

W*hy Churches Die*. *(2007)* **ISBN 978-1-9796019-03** A fresh assessment of congregational vitality to determine thirty-five reasons why faith-based congregations were losing their pristine power of outreach.

Interpreting an Author's Words. *(2008)* **ISBN 978-0980-164-74** —Define both formal and informal study and writing skills by understanding how to clearly interpret the spoken and written words of others.

Titanic Lesson. *(2008)* **ISBN 978-0-9796019-6-5** -- An answer to the question: "Do historic realities predict problems for a growing faith-based group?

Sympathetic Leadership Cybernetics. *(2010)* **ISBN 978-1-9354345-28** – This work attempts to clarify management and leadership in the context of organizational and institutional functionality and charts a course for organizations to serve the needs of people through shepherd management and servant leadership.

Why Christianity Fails in America. (2010) **ISBN 978-0-9796019-10**-- A call for an internal redirection of the heart and soul to make the pristine faith viable in the Twenty-first century.

How to Build a Better Spouse Trap. *(2010)* **ISBN 978-1-9354344-50** – A major failure of faith-based groups is they have made little difference in the lives of individuals and their function in the family. How to choose a mate, learn for our mistakes, stay married, and teach others to break the cycle of dysfunctional relationships. The family unit is a microcosm of faith-based behavior.

Discipleship. *(2010) ISBN* **978-0-9796019-5-8**--A revived edition to better explain the process of a believer's lifestyle from conversion (change direction), to discipleship (learning), to apostle (mature enough to be trusted with the message grace.)

SO TALES. *(2011)* **ISBN 978-1-9354345-80** -- Preserving true 240 true stories from the past for the benefit of family and friends.

Designing Valid Research. *(2011)* **ISBN 978-1-9354345-73** – A guide to designing a research proposal and developing a social scientific dissertation.

Titanic Lessons. *(2012)* **ISBN 978-0-9796019-6-5** – An effort to demonstrate that bigger is not necessarily better and that all building of machines, organizations, and institutions must use material that meets the precise requirements of the task. This must be applied to people, process, and functionality of the human element and the mechanics must match the environment.

Why Wait Till Sunday? (2012) **ISBN 978-1-935434-27-6**-- A renewal plan for older congregations who depended on programs coming down from sectarian authority rather than locally generated ideas and involvement in seven (7) aspects of renewal.

Fighting the Amalekites. *(2013)* **ISBN 978-1-935434-30-6** – The unhealthy addictions, unproductive habits, an uncontrolled tongue are all little "Amalekites" unless these are destroyed they will become the destroyer. These join the Amalekites that ambush and take advantage of spiritual weaknesses.

Remedial and Surrogate Parenting *(2013)* **ISBN 978-1-9354344-81** --Children are a gift of God and a legacy of faith-based families; therefore, parenting skills are an essential aspect of religion. This work is guidance for remedial human development (0-20) for parents, teachers, and childcare workers.

Transformational Leadership in Education. *(2013) Second Edition ISBN* **978-1-9354342-38**-- *A* strengths-based approach to education for administrators, teachers, and guidance counselors.

Tear Down These Walls. (2013) **ISBN 978-1-9354341-84** -- A priority agenda must be to make people moral citizens of the world before they can become mystical citizens of heaven. Where organized groups choose not to function, personal action could make a difference and break down some of the barriers that divide the faith-based community and strengthen the "One Lord-One Faith–One Baptism" message.

The EVERGREEN Devotional New Testament – C.A.F.E. Edition. *(2015, 2019)* **ISBN 978-1-9354342-69** – *EDNT is a* 42-year project to translate common NT Greek and determine the meaning "then" and how words can best be expressed "now" and remain true to the original intent expressed in a common devotional language.

Recycled Words n' Stuff. *(2016)* ISBN **978-1-9354348-63** – A collection of short narratives and essays of general interest.

The Children's Bread –*unlocking whole life stewardship* (2018) **ISBN 978-1-935434-90-0**– *Appreciating faith-based* economics and personal wealth to unlock a missional lifestyle and f0unding for humanitarian and faith-based entities.

Kingdom Growth Through Missional Behavior *(2019)—adopting the thinking, behaviors, and practices of a missionary in order to globalize the message of grace* **ISBN 978-1-935434-91-7**

God Has Confidence in You (2019) "they lived incaves and holes in the earth and obtained a od report through faith..."**ISBN 978-1-930839-04-9**

Power of Forgiveness and Reconciliation (2020) Forgiveness Is The Sunrise of Reconciliation. *(See Appendix D)* For more data on The Power Series see Appendix E. **ISBN978-1-950839-06-3**

Beyond Pulpit, Classroom and Lecture Hall (2020) -- *Unlocking Exposition, Instruction an Research Reporting in Subject Matter Sharing.* **ISBN 978-1-950839-03-2**

Research Methods for Problem Solvers and Critical Thinkers. *(2021)* --Guidance in development a master's thesis, designing a doctoral research proposal and constructing a defendable dissertation based on social scientific research with an objective of positive social change. **ISBN 978-1-950839-XX-X**

All Believers are Converted Equal (2021) *–Developing the Path to Moral Excellence. (Based on 2 Peter Chapter One.* **ISBN 978-1-950839-XX-X**

(See www.gea-books.com/bookstore*)*
or anywhere good books are sold.

Selected Reference Bibliography

Adams, Marilyn McCord, 1991, "Forgiveness: A Christian Model", *Faith and Philosophy*, 8(3): 277–304. doi:10.5840/faithphil19918319

Allais, Lucy, 2008, "Wiping the Slate Clean: The Heart of Forgiveness", *Philosophy and Public Affairs*, 36(1): 33–68. doi:10.1111/j.1088-4963.2008.00123.x

Anderson, David A. 2010. Gracism: The Art of Inclusion, Bridge Leader Books.

Arendt, Hannah, 1958, *The Human Condition*, Chicago: University of Chicago Press.

Aristotle, *Nicomachean Ethics*, in the *The Complete Works of Aristotle*, The Revised Oxford Translation, vol. 2, Jonathan Barnes (ed.), Princeton: Princeton University Press, 1984.

Austin, J.L., [1962] 1975, *How to Do Things with Words*, 2nd edition, J.O. Urmson and Marina Sbisá (eds.), Cambridge, MA: Harvard University Press (first edition 1962).

Bash, Anthony, 2007, *Forgiveness and Christian Ethics*, Cambridge: Cambridge University Press.

—, 2015, *Forgiveness: A Theology*, Eugene: Cascade Books.

Bell, Macalester, 2008, "Forgiving Someone for Who They Are (and Not Just What They've Done)", *Philosophy and Phenomenological Research*, 77(3): 625–658. doi:10.1111/j.1933-1592.2008.00213.x

Biggar, Nigel, 2008, "Forgiving Enemies in Ireland", *Journal of Religious Ethics*, 36(4): 559–579. doi:10.1111/j.1467-9795.2008.00362.x

Blustein, Jeffrey M., 2014, *Forgiveness and Remembrance: Remembering Wrongdoing in Personal and Public Life*, New York: Oxford University Press.

Boon, Susan D. and Lorne M. Sulsky, 1997, "Attributions of Blame and Forgiveness in Romantic Relationships: A Policy-capturing Study", *Journal of Social Behavior and Personality*, 12(1): 19–44.

Brien, Andrew, 1989, "Can God Forgive Us our Trespasses?" *Sophia*, 28(2): 35–42. doi:10.1007/BF02789857

Darby, Bruce W. and Barry R. Schlenker, 1982, "Children's Reactions to Apologies", *Journal of Personality and Social Psychology*, 43(4): 742–753. doi:10.1037/0022-3514.43.4.742

Darwall, Stephen, 2006, *The Second-Person Standpoint: Morality, Respect, and Accountability*, Cambridge, MA: Harvard University Press.

de Waal, Frans B.M. and Jen .J. Pokorny, 2005, "Primate Conflict and Its Relation to Human Forgiveness", in Everett L. Worthington (Ed.). *Handbook of Forgiveness*, New York: Brunner-Routledge, pp. 15–32.

Drabkin, Douglas, 1993, "The Nature of God's Love and Forgiveness", *Religious Studies*, 29(2): 231–238. doi:10.1017/S0034412500022228

Emerson, James G., 1964, *The Dynamics of Forgiveness*, Philadelphia: Westminster Press.

Enright, Robert D., David L. Eastin, Sandra Golden, Issidoros Sarinopoulos, and Suzanne Freedman, 1992, "Interpersonal Forgiveness Within the Helping Profession: An Attempt to Resolve Differences of Opinion", *Counseling and Values*, 36(2): 84–103. doi:10.1002/j.2161-007X.1991.tb00966.x

Enright, Robert D. and Richard P. Fitzgibbons, 2000, *Helping Clients Forgive: An Empirical Guide for Resolving Anger and Restoring Hope*, Washington, DC: American Psychological Association.

Fricke, Christel (ed.), 2011, *The Ethics of Forgiveness*, New York: Routledge.

Garcia, Ernesto V., 2011, "Bishop Butler on Forgiveness and Resentment", *Philosophers' Imprint*, 11(10): 1–19. [Garcia 2011 available online]

Garrard, Eve and David McNaughton, 2002, "In Defense of Unconditional Forgiveness", *Proceedings of the Aristotelian Society*, 103(1): 39–60. doi:10.1111/j.0066-7372.2003.00063.x

Gavrilyuk, Paul L., 2004, *The Suffering of the Impassible God: The Dialectics of Patristic Thought*, Oxford: Oxford University Press. doi:10.1093/0199269823.001.0001

Gert, Bernard, 2010, *Hobbes: Prince of Peace*, Cambridge: Polity.

Gordon, Kristina Coop, Donald H. Baucom, and Douglas K. Snyder, 2000, "The Use of Forgiveness in Marital Therapy", in McCullough, Pargament, and Thoresen 2000: 203–227

Govier, Trudy, 2002, *Forgiveness and Revenge*, London: Routledge.

Green, Barton L., 2009. Between *the Lines and Spaces* Standard, Cincinnati.

Green, Hollis L. 2010. Why Christianity Fails in America.. GlobalEdAdvancePRESS. Nashville

Green, Hollis L. 2013. Transformational Leadership in Education. GlobalEdAdvancePRESS. Nashville

Green, Hollis L. 2013. Tear Down These Walls, GlobalEdAdvancePRESS. Nashville

Green, Hollis L. 2013. Fighting the Amalekites. GlobalEdAdvancePRESS. Nashville

Green, Hollis L. 2018. The Children's Bread, GlobalEdAdvancePRESS. Nashville

Green, Hollis L. 2019. Kingdom Growth Through Missional Behavior. GlobalEdAdvancePRESS. Nashville

Griswold, Charles L., 2007, *Forgiveness: A Philosophical Exploration*, New York: Cambridge University Press.

Griswold, Charles L., Konstan, David (eds.). *Ancient Forgiveness, Classical, Judaic, and Christian.* (2011). Cambridge University Press.

Hallich, Oliver, 2013, "Can the Paradox of Forgiveness Be Dissolved?" *Ethical Theory and Moral Practice*, 16(5): 999–1017.doi:10.1007/s10677-012-9400-5

Haji, Ishtiyaque and Justin Caouette (eds.), 2013, *Free Will and Moral Responsibility*, Newcastle upon Tyne: Cambridge Scholars Press.

Hoffman, Karen D., 2009, "Forgiveness Without Apology: Defending Unconditional Forgiveness", *Proceedings of the American Catholic Philosophical Association*, 82: 135–151. doi:10.5840/acpaproc20088210

Holmgren, Margaret R., 1993, "Forgiveness and the Intrinsic Value of Persons", *American Philosophical Quarterly*, 30(4): 341–352.

–––, 2012, *Forgiveness and Retribution: Responding to Wrongdoing*, Cambridge: Cambridge University Press.

Ingram, Stephen, 2013, "The Prudential Value of Forgiveness", *Philosophia*, 41(4): 1069–1078.

Kekes, John, 2009, "Blame Versus Forgiveness", *The Monist*, 92(4): 488–506. doi:10.5840/monist200992428

Konstan, David, 2010, *Before Forgiveness: Origins of a Moral Idea*, Cambridge: Cambridge University Press.

Malcolm, Wanda M. and Leslie S. Greenberg, 2000, "Forgiveness as a Process of Change in Individual Psychotherapy", in McCullough, Pargament, and Thoresen 2000: 179–202

McCullough, Michael E., 2008, *Beyond Revenge: The Evolution of the Forgiveness Instinct*, San Francisco: Jossey-Bass.

Milam, Per-Erik, 2015, "How is Self-Forgiveness Possible?" *Pacific Philosophical Quarterly*, 96(1): 49–69. doi:10.1111/papq.12091

Novitz, David, 1998, "Forgiveness and Self-Respect", *Philosophy and Phenomenological Research*, 58(2): 299–315. doi:10.2307/2653510

Nussbaum, Martha, 2016, *Anger and Forgiveness: Resentment, Generosity, Justice*, New York: Oxford University Press.

Pettigrove, Glen, 2004a, "The Forgiveness We Speak: The Illocutionary Force of Forgiving", *The Southern Journal of Philosophy*, 42(3): 371–392. doi:10.1111/j.2041-6962.2004.tb01938.x

———, 2012, *Forgiveness and Love*, Oxford: Oxford University Press.

———, 2010, "Moral Bystanders and the Virtue of Forgiveness", In Christopher R. Allers and Marieke Smit (eds.), *Forgiveness in Perspective*, Amsterdam: Rodopi, pp. 66–69.

Richards, Norvin, 1988, "Forgiveness", *Ethics*, 99(1): 77–97. doi:10.1086/293036

Roberts, Robert C., 1995, "Forgivingness", *American Philosophical Quarterly*, 32(4): 289–306.

Scarre, Geoffrey, 2004, *After Evil: Responding to Wrongdoing*, Burlington, VT: Ashgate.

Smith, Nick, 2008, *I Was Wrong: The Meanings of Apologies*, Cambridge: Cambridge University Press.

Snow, Nancy E., 1992, "Se000lf-Forgiveness", *Journal of Value Inquiry*, 27(1): 57–65. doi:10.1007/BF01082713

Tombs, David, 2008, "The Offer of Forgiveness", *Journal of Religious Ethics*, 36(4): 587–593. doi:0.1111/j.1467-9795.2008.00363_2.x

Tutu, Desmond, 1999, *No Future Without Forgiveness*, New York: Random House.

Walker, Margaret Urban, 2013, "Third Parties and the Social Scaffolding of Forgiveness", *Journal of Religious Ethics*, 41(3): 495–512. doi:10.1111/jore.12026

Ware, Owen, 2014, "Forgiveness and Respect for Persons", *American Philosophical Quarterly*, 51(3): 247–260.

——, 2016b, "The Normative Significance of Forgiveness", *Australasian Journal of Philosophy*, 94(4): 687–703. doi:10.1080/00048402.2015.1126850

Warmke, Brandon and Michael McKenna, 2013, "Moral Responsibility, Forgiveness, and Conversation", in Haji and Caouette 2013: 189–212.

Weiner, Bernard, Sandra Graham, Orli Peter, and Mary Zmuidinas, 1991, "Public Confession and Forgiveness", *Journal of Personality*, 59(2): 281–312. doi:10.1111/j.1467-6494.1991.tb00777.x

Williston, Byron, 2012, "The Importance of Self-Forgiveness", *American Philosophical Quarterly*, 49(1): 67–80.

Wilson, John, 1988, "Why Forgiveness Requires Repentance", *Philosophy*, 63(246): 534–535. doi:10.1017/S0031819100043850

Wolterstorff, Nicholas, 2009, "Jesus and Forgiveness", In *Jesus and Philosophy: New Essays*, Paul K. Moser (ed.), Cambridge: Cambridge University Press, pp.

www.ingramcontent.com/pod-product-compliance
Lightning Source LLC
Chambersburg PA
CBHW061308110426
42742CB00012BA/2104